EUROPEAN JOURNAL OF WORK AND
ORGANIZATIONAL PSYCHOLOGY
2006, 15 (2), 129–138

After work is done: Psychological perspectives on recovery from work

Fred R. H. Zijlstra

Department of Psychology, School of Human Sciences, University of Surrey, Guildford, UK

Sabine Sonnentag

Work and Organizational Psychology, Department of Psychology, University of Konstanz, Konstanz, Germany

INTRODUCTION

Research on the relation between work and health has primarily focused on the effects of psychosocial characteristics of the job (i.e., autonomy, psychological demands) on psychological well-being and other health-related outcomes. However, in the last decade the awareness has risen that an integral part of a healthy life is an adequate balance between work and private life (work–life balance, work-family balance; cf. Jones, Burke, & Westman, 2005). Part of a healthy life style is recovering from the daily strains. The topic of recovery from work has not received much scientific attention, and consequently the process of recovery is not yet well understood (for reviews, cf. Eden, 2001a, 2001b). With this special issue we want to contribute to the understanding of the process of recovery, and we hope that this issue will help to put this topic on the research agenda. This special issue presents a selection of articles that look into different aspects related to recovery, such as aspects that are work-related and aspects that are related to the time after work. In this introduction we will outline some background information that is needed to position the concept of

Correspondence should be addressed to Professor Fred R. H. Zijlstra, Faculty of Psychology, Maastricht University, P.O. Box 616, NL 6200 MD Maastricht, The Netherlands. E-mail: fred.zijlstra@psychology.unimaas.nl

http://www.psypress.com/ejwop   DOI: 10.1080/13594320500513855

recovery, and to highlight the psychological perspectives on recovery. First, we will discuss the relation of recovery with fatigue, and then we will present the "cycle of work and rest". Subsequently, we will address the relationship between work characteristics and recovery and will describe the relevance of leisure and sleep.

FATIGUE AND RECOVERY

Intuitively it is evident that after a period of work people need some rest to recover. During the working day people are confronted with all kind of demands, ranging from physical and cognitive to emotional demands. Dealing with these demands requires physical work, attention, and concentration, in short expending physical and/or mental energy. Energy expenditure is what makes people feel fatigued by the end of the working day because their resources are depleted, both in energetic and emotional respect (cf. Meijman, Mulder, & van Dormolen, 1992). These feelings of fatigue require people to take a rest in order to recuperate from their effort investments and to allow their resources to be replenished. This process of replenishing resources is usually indicated as "recovery". Recovery is important because it allows people to prepare and be ready for new challenges (i.e., another day at work), and it will prevent accumulation of fatigue that ultimately can lead to serious health consequences.

From a conceptual point of view, recovery should be seen as a *process* that allows us to replenish our resources. In essence this is what we do when we take a rest or go to sleep. The implication of taking a rest is that one is (temporary) relieved of the demands, and this relief will allow to replenish the resources that have been used. The anticipated effect of the recovery process is reduction of fatigue. In *physiological* sense this implies that the organism is allowed to "unwind", which actually means that the arousal level (as indicated by adrenaline excretion rate and heart rate) is allowed to return to a "baseline level" again (Craig & Cooper, 1992). The *psychological* effects to be anticipated are that people feel capable and ready to continue with the current demands or to meet new demands. A common expression referring to this effect is "charging the batteries". This means that work and rest need to alternate and should constitute a "cycle of work and rest".

However, for various reasons it is not always feasible to take a rest, thus other options need to be explored. In many cases changing activities has a similar effect as taking a rest, because a change in activities is often accompanied by a change in demands (e.g., alternating physical activities with mental activities). As a consequence different resources are used (e.g., muscles vs. "brain power"). In fact this is what people actually do: after work they engage in various types of activities, varying from household activities and childcare to sports and leisure.

CYCLE OF WORK AND REST

The "cycle of work and rest" is primarily determined by the working times. While at work people are not supposed to rest; resting is what they should do in their "own time". The lunch and coffee/tea breaks are illustrations of this: Employers usually do not pay salary over lunch breaks. Working times are therefore important; they specify when people have to be at work, and when they are "free to go". The time "after work" traditionally is the time in which people should be able to recover from the daily strains at work. This pattern in principle repeats itself every day, and therefore is referred as the "cycle of work and rest". However, the time after work is not only for recovery. Many people have commitments and duties after work and are not entirely free to spend their time. Some of these commitments and duties will place additional demands upon people and some of these demands will be similar to work demands, while other activities have entirely different demands. The question is how these demands interact with the demands of work: Are they to be added on top of the work demands or do they compensate for the work demands? Already in the late 1970s, Piotrkowsky (1978) reported that some workers were just too drained by physical tiredness or by working in boring jobs that they developed apathy for family life and other activities. Although numerous things have changed over the last decades, such as the fact that work nowadays is primarily mentally demanding rather than physically demanding (Zijlstra, Schalk, & Roe, 1996), yet the number of people complaining about work pressure and fatigue is still high (Paoli & Merllié, 2001). Paoli and Merllié reported on a survey among the working population in Europe. Their results indicate that more than half of the working population in Europe complained about having to work under pressure (i.e., either working at high speed, or having to meet tight deadlines). Occupationally induced fatigue, i.e., the short-term effect of a working day, is a common complaint, affecting about 25–33% of the working population in the Netherlands (Bultmann et al., 2002). The fatigue people experience may have an effect on what kind of activities they are willing to undertake after work. People may decide that they are too tired for certain activities or initiatives and thus stay at home and resort to a passive type of leisure (i.e., watching television).

Working times are not only important in terms of work and rest, but they are one of the first and most important aspects of work organisation: It synchronizes people's presence and therefore facilitates any form of organizing and cooperation. In particular since the industrial revolution, when mass-production in factory plants started, the regulation of working times has become an issue. One of the consequences of regulated working times is that people have less influence over the decisions of when to work and when to take a break—nowadays the majority of employees have no flexibility, or decision authority, with respect to their working times. In addition, people sometimes have to work extra hours, and this may affect the cycle of work and rest.

Recent technological developments have had an impact on working times. Internet and mobile communication facilities allow people to work from wherever they want, and whenever they choose to work. This development has introduced the phenomenon of "tele-homework" and "distance work", which in fact has decreased the importance of working times (Roe et al., 1994). Working late in the evening necessarily reduces the opportunity for recovery. Rau and Triemer (2004) found that people who regularly worked overtime had more sleep problems than those who worked regular hours. However, people in that study worked in their official work place and not at home. Studies on (tele-)homework suggest that the boundaries between work and private life tend to diminish (Ahrentzen, 1990), and that as a result people find themselves working late night. Some people complain that it feels as if they are never finished. So, from a recovery point of view this seems to have undesirable consequences; it evidently affects the daily work – rest cycle. Apparently the boundaries between work and home have an important psychological function: They help people to create a psychological distance between work and themselves, which is necessary to unwind. When these boundaries between work and home become less clear people seem not able to distance themselves from the demands being imposed upon them, and therefore will have difficulties disengaging themselves from work (see Cropley, Dijk, & Stanley, 2006 this issue; Sonnentag & Kruel, 2006 this issue).

Yet there are many interesting questions related to the cycle of work and rest, and thus to the topic of recovery, such as "what is the optimum period for work and for rest?", "what factors facilitate recovery?", "how does recovery impact on subsequent work behaviour"? "How should jobs be designed so that recovery is facilitated?", "What is the role of sleep with respect to recovery from work"? And more questions could be formulated.

WORK CHARACTERISTICS AND RECOVERY

As indicated above working times and thus the length of the working day determine people's opportunity to recover. However, the characteristics of the job itself also appear to have an effect on recovery. The extent to which people can "switch off" from work in the evening seems to be important. Studies have indicated that the intensity of the working day plays a role in this respect. For example, Meijman et al. (1992) have demonstrated that people working in intensive working conditions have more difficulties in unwinding during the evening compared to people who do similar work but face less intensive conditions. Furthermore, the level of autonomy at work is important because it allows people to regulate their own work speed (Jackson, Wall, Martin, & Davids, 1993), and therefore also their own level of effort investment (cf.

Zijlstra, 1993; Zijlstra, Roe, Leonova, & Krediet, 1999). In general one could say that when work is very demanding, for example when it is characterized by high levels of responsibility or high work pressure, it can cause a feeling of strain, which in itself leads to a greater need for recovery (Sluiter, van-der-Beek, & Frings-Dresen, 1999), but may also make it more difficult for individuals to unwind after work (Sonnentag & Bayer, 2005). This means that the nature of the working day has an effect on the type of activities people engage in after work. Optimal recovery from work is dependent on the opportunity and time for recovery and the type and quality of activities people pursue (Sonnentag, 2001; Sonnentag & Zijlstra, 2006).

LEISURE AND RECOVERY

Most people in our society consider work to be the dominant activity and leisure as being trivial. This view on work and leisure is a consequence of what is called the Puritan (or Protestant) work ethic, in which work is glorified and leisure is devalued. In such situations leisure becomes a derivate of work, solely used for recuperation and distraction (Hunnicut, 1988). However, the essence of leisure is "perceived freedom and intrinsic motivation" to engage in activities (Iso-Ahola, 1980). This view is in strong contrast to most work situations, where people's activities are usually externally prescribed and regulated, and perceived as an obligatory duty. At work people have a contractual obligation to be present and perform particular activities. Also, other activities that people engage in during "after work time" are not always intrinsically motivated, but people do engage in these activities out of their free will; there is no contractual obligation.

Some people see the merits of leisure in its own right (Iso-Ahola, 1997). Leisure activities can, like work, have beneficial effects on mental health and personality development (see also Rau, 2006 this issue). In societies that do not value leisure, people are not able to reconcile work and family, have little time for cultivating hobbies, and find it difficult to engage in civic activities that would nourish a democratic society. Also from a psychological perspective it would be better if people engaged in activities in which they sought challenges and tried to match them with their skills. Evidently this also applies to work: Optimal experiences correlate positively with mental health (Csikszentmihalyi, 1990).

However, in our society leisure is used as an "escape" from work. "Escapism" in this respect means that people do not seek meaningful leisure activities for their own growth and development, but, instead, resort to passive activities to escape from everyday strains and problems. Such behaviour is frequently associated with a passive lifestyle and boredom, which in turn might feed into apathy and depression. From this perspective is it rather worrisome that watching television seems to be the dominant activity for many people in their "after work time". Schor (1991) referred to this as part of the "work-spend-work-spend" mentality that seems to be prevalent in our society.

SLEEP AND RECOVERY

Sleep plays a very important role in the process of recovery. It is assumed that sleep must be continuous in order to be restorative (Walsh & Lindeblom, 2000). Sleep loss and sleep disturbance can lead to mood changes, fatigue, and performance decrement and in extreme cases even to immune function impairment (Harrison & Horne, 1999). Even moderate sleep loss is associated with deficits in alertness and performance (Åkerstedt, Knutsson et al., 2002; Dinges et al., 1997). Lack of sleep or poor quality of sleep is also associated with absenteeism, reduced productivity, and an increased risk of fatigue-related accidents (Åkerstedt, Fredlund et al., 2002; Stoller, 1994). Lack of sleep or disrupted sleep can result in not feeling refreshed the in the morning. When people are not refreshed this suggests that they haven't completely recovered, and are not in an optimal condition to meet new demands and challenges. Work will then cost extra effort (Zijlstra, 1993). The implication is that lack of recovery can lead to accumulation of fatigue and strain and ultimately can cause health problems.

Most studies in the domain of work and health have neglected the area of sleep. This is surprising considering the association between high work demands and sleep disturbance (Åkerstedt, Knutsson et al., 2002; Cropley, Steptoe, & Joekes, 1999). However, the mechanisms by which occupational stress is associated with sleep disturbance are not yet fully understood. One possibility may be that people in stressful jobs are very active during the evening and therefore are too physiologically aroused at bedtime what causes difficulties in falling asleep. They need to "unwind" first. Another possibility is that people may have difficulties in "switching off" from work-related issues and thoughts at bedtime, and thus still ruminate about the problems at work and thus have difficulties in falling asleep. Harvey (2000) showed that presleep cognition affects sleep quality, and manipulations of cognitive arousal before sleep leads to longer sleep latencies (Gross & Borkovec, 1982).

In particular when people have problems to deal with at work or when they experience conflicts at work, people may have ruminative thoughts, which make it difficult to switch off from work. A recent survey on sleep behaviour found that about 17% of a representative sample of the working population in the UK reported that they have sleeping problems caused by worrying about their work (Groeger, Zijlstra, & Dijk, 2004). Studies have shown that a failure to unwind after work leads to sleep complaints, and consequently makes people feel not-refreshed the next morning (Meijman et al., 1992; Sluiter et al., 1999). Thus, sleep problems are associated with fatigue, and can have an impact on recovery.

THIS ISSUE

Health and well-being are related to both people's work and leisure activities. Mental health problems (e.g., psychological complaints such as burnout, depressive feelings, and stress-related complaints) are currently the fastest-growing category mentioned among long term absentees from work, indicating that this is a serious problem. As individuals' energetic resources are not infinite, they have to recover form time to time.

Although there is increasing evidence that the process of recovery is important for a healthy and balanced life (cf. Gump & Matthews, 2000), this process has not yet received the scientific attention it deserves. A few studies have looked into the effects of holidays and vacations (Fritz & Sonnentag, in press; Strauss-Blasche, Muhry, Lehofer, Moser, & Markl, 2004; Westman & Eden, 1997; Westman & Etzion, 2001). These studies have indicated that vacations have a beneficial effect on well-being; however, these effects are usually short lived. A more structural solution is desirable, and this requires a better understanding of the process of recovery. It is intuitively clear that sleep is important for recovery, although the exact mechanisms and processes in this respect are not entirely clear yet. There are indications that day time activities also have an effect on recovery. The question is whether daytime activities affect recovery because they affect people's sleep or whether they have an effect in their own right. But there are more questions that need to be answered, such as "what are the determinants of optimal recovery?" and "how do activities during the day affect the recovery process?"

This issue presents five articles that address various aspects related to recovery. One important topic refers to the extent to which job characteristics are associated with recovery. The study by Taris and colleagues focuses on the aspects of working times and deals with the question whether contract working time and overtime may affect the opportunities for recovery, and thus may reduce recovery. Analyses showed that in a sample of managers contract working hours were negatively related to exhaustion. Overtime was positively related to work enjoyment, but also to time-based work home interference.

Cropley and colleagues address the issue of the association between job strain and sleep quality. The article provides evidence that people working in high strain jobs need longer to unwind after work and ruminate more about work-related issues. The study also demonstrates that there is a positive association between high strain jobs and sleeping problems.

The article by Rau reports findings from a study that included physiological data. The study provided evidence that job incumbents whose jobs are well-designed and who have opportunities to develop themselves are better off not only in terms of mental health, but also in terms of recovery. Analyses showed that high learning opportunities—as assessed by behavioural data—were positively related to a pronounced decline of heart rate and blood pressure during the night. Such a decline is a strong indicator for successful cardiovascular recovery.

The article by Sonnentag and Kruel presents a study that examined the relation between job stressors and people's ability to switch off after work. Specifically, the study showed that teachers experiencing a high workload had more difficulties "switching off" from work during the evening. Interestingly, this relationship is not only based on self-report data but is also reflected in observations provided by family members. Together the articles by Cropley and colleagues, Rau, as well as Sonnentag and Kruel suggest that work characteristics encountered during the day extends its effect during the after-work period and affects the recovery process.

The article by Rook and Zijlstra presents a study on the weekly pattern of fatigue and sleep quality, and examines the contribution of various activities towards recovery. Sport activities turned out to be negatively associated with fatigue. Interesting to note is that people apparently seem to anticipate the strain of the working week, given the fact that the lowest sleep quality is found on Monday morning. This finding suggests that recovery is a highly complex process in which also anticipatory and expectation processes play an important role (Eden, 2001b).

Thus, as a whole the studies present a complex picture of work and recovery. Important factors that potentially impact on recovery and opportunities for recovery include workload as well as aspects of job control and learning requirements. Recovery itself is reflected in psychological detachment from work, low fatigue, as well as sleep and decrease in physiological parameters during the night.

Recovery from work is an important topic. Articles in this issue illustrate that when work and organizational psychologists want to learn more about people's well-being they also need to look at "after-work time". This special issue certainly does not pretend to answer all the questions that have been formulated, but we do hope that it stimulates further investigations on this important topic.

REFERENCES

Ahrentzen, S. B. (1990). Managing conflict by managing boundaries: How professional homeworkers cope with multiple roles at home. *Environment and Behavior, 22*, 723–752.

Åkerstedt, T., Fredlund, P., Gillberg, M., & Jansson, B. (2002). A prospective study of fatal occupational accidents—relationship to sleeping difficulties and occupational factors. *Journal of Sleep Research, 11*, 69–71.

Åkerstedt, T., Knutsson, A., Westerholm, P., Theorell, T., Alfredsson, L., & Kecklund, G. (2002). Sleep disturbances, work stress and work hours: A cross-sectional study. *Journal of Psychosomatic Research, 53*, 741–748.

Bultmann, U., Kant, I., Kasl, S. V., Schroer, K. A. P., Swaen, G. M. H., & van den Brandt, P. A. (2002). Lifestyle factors as risk factors for fatigue and psychological distress in the working population: Prospective results from the Maastricht Cohort Study. *Journal of Occupational and Environmental Medicine, 44*, 116–124.

Craig, A., & Cooper, R. E. (1992). Symptoms of acute and chronic fatigue. In A. P. Smith & D. M. Jones (Eds.), *Handbook of human performance* (Vol. 3, pp. 289–339). London: Academic Press.

Cropley, M., Dijk, D.-J., & Stanley, N. (2006). Job strain, work rumination, and sleep in school teachers. *European Journal of Work and Organizational Psychology, 15*(2), 181–196.

Cropley, M., Steptoe, A., & Joekes, K. (1999). Job strain and psychiatric morbidity. *Psychological Medicine, 29*, 1411–1416.

Csikszentmihalyi, M. (1990). *Flow*. New York: Harper & Row.

Dinges, D. F., Pack, F., Williams, K., Gillen, K. A., Powell, J. W., Ott, G. E., et al. (1997). Cumulative sleepiness, mood disturbance, and psychomotor vigilance performance decrements during a week of sleep restricted to 4–5 hours per night. *Sleep, 20*, 267–277.

Eden, D. (2001a). Job stress and respite relief: Overcoming high-tech tethers. In P. L. Perrewé & D. C. Ganster (Eds.), *Research in occupational stress and well-being: Exploring theoretical mechanisms and perspectives* (pp. 143–194). Amsterdam: JAI Press.

Eden, D. (2001b). Vacations and other respites: Studying stress on and off the job. In C. Cooper & I. Robertson (Eds.), *Well-being in organisations: A reader for students and practitioners* (pp. 121–146). Chichester, UK: Wiley.

Fritz, C., & Sonnentag, S. (in press). Recovery, well-being, and performance-related outcomes: The role of workload and vacation experiences. *Journal of Applied Psychology*.

Groeger, J. A., Zijlstra, F. R. H., & Dijk, D.-J. (2004). Sleep quantity, sleep difficulties and their perceived consequences in a representative sample of some two thousand British adults. *Journal of Sleep Research, 13*, 359–371.

Gross, R. T., & Borkovec, T. D. (1982). The effects of a cognitive intrusion manipulation on the sleep-onset latency of good sleepers. *Behaviour Therapy, 13*, 112–116.

Gump, B., & Matthews, K. (2000). Are vacations food for your health? A 9-year mortality experience after the multiple risk factor intervention trial. *Psychosomatic Medicine, 62*, 608–612.

Harrison, Y., & Horne, J. A. (1999). One night of sleep loss impairs innovative thinking and flexible decision making. *Organizational Behavior and Human Decision Processes, 78*, 128–145.

Harvey, A. G. (2000). Pre-sleep cognitive activity: A comparison of sleep-onset insomniacs and good sleepers. *British Journal of Clinical Psychology, 39*, 275–286.

Hunnicut, B. (1988). *Work without end: Abandoning of shorter hours for the right to work*. Philadelphia: Temple University Press.

Iso-Ahola, S. (1980). *The social psychology of leisure and recreation*. Dubuque, IA: W.C. Brown.

Iso-Ahola, S. (1997). A psychological analysis of leisure and health. In J. T. Haworth (Ed.), *Work, leisure and well-being* (pp. 131–144). London: Routledge.

Jackson, P. R., Wall, T. D., Martin, R., & Davids, K. (1993). New measures of job control, cognitive demand, and production responsibility. *Journal of Applied Psychology, 78*, 753–762.

Jones, F., Burke, R., & Westman, M. (Eds.). (2005). *Work–life balance: A psychological perspective*. Hove, UK: Psychology Press.

Meijman, T. F., Mulder, G., & van Dormolen, M. (1992). Workload of driving examiners: A psychophysiological field study. In H. Kragt (Ed.), *Enhancing industrial performances* (pp. 245–260). London: Taylor & Francis.

Paoli, P., & Merllié, D. (2001). *Third European survey on working conditions 2000*. Dublin: European Foundation for the Improvement of Working and Living Conditions. Retrieved from http://www.eurofound.eu.int/publications/files/EF9721EN.pdf

Piotrkowski, C. S. (1978). *Work and the family system*. New York: Free Press.

Rau, R. (2006). Learning opportunities at work as predictor for recovery and health. *European Journal of Work and Organizational Psychology, 15*(2), 158–180.

Rau, R., & Triemer, A. (2004). Overtime in relation to blood pressure and mood during work, leisure, and night time. *Social Indicators Research, 67*, 51–73.

Roe, R. A., van den Berg, P. T., Zijlstra, F. R. H., Schalk, M. J. D., Taillieu, T. C. B., & van der Wielen, J. M. M. (1994). New concepts for a new age: Information service organizations and mental information work. *The European Work and Organizational Psychologist, 3*, 177–192.

Rook, J. W., & Zijlstra, F. R. H. (2006). The contribution of various types of activities to recovery. *European Journal of Work and Organizational Psychology, 15*(2), 218–240.

Schor, J. (1991). *The overworked American: The unexpected decline of leisure*. New York: Basic Books.

Sluiter, J. K., van-der-Beek, A. J., & Frings-Dresen, M. H. V. (1999). The influences of work characteristics on the need for recovery and experienced health: A study on coach drivers. *Ergonomics, 42*, 573–583.

Sonnentag, S. (2001). Work, recovery activities, and individual well-being: A diary study. *Journal of Occupational Health Psychology, 6*, 196–210.

Sonnentag, S., & Bayer, U.-V. (2005). Switching off mentally: Predictors and consequences of psychological detachment from work during off-job time. *Journal of Occupational Health Psychology, 10*, 393–414.

Sonnentag, S., & Kruel, U. (2006). Psychological detachment from work during off-job time: The role of job stressors, job involvement, and recovery-related self-efficacy. *European Journal of Work and Organizational Psychology, 15*(2), 197–217.

Sonnentag, S., & Zijlstra, F. R. H. (2006). Job characteristics and off-job time activities as predictors for need for recovery, well-being, and fatigue. *Journal of Applied Psychology, 91*, 123–142.

Stoller, M. K. (1994). Economic effects of insomnia. *Clinical Therapy, 16*, 873–897.

Strauss-Blasche, G., Muhry, F., Lehofer, M., Moser, M., & Markl, W. (2004). Time course of well-being after a three-week resort-based respite from occupational and domestic demands: Carry-over, contrast and situation effects. *Journal of Leisure Research, 36*, 293–309.

Taris, T. W., Beckers, D., Verhoeven, L. C., Geurts, S. A. E., Kompier, M. A. J., & van der Linden, D. (2006). Recovery opportunities, work–home interference, and well-being among managers. *European Journal of Work and Organizational Psychology, 15*(2), 139–157.

Walsh, J. K., & Lindblom, S. S. (2000). Psychophysiology of sleep deprivation and disruption. In M. R. Pressman & W. C. Orr (Eds.), *Understanding sleep: The evaluation and treatment of sleep disorders* (pp. 73–110). Washington, DC: APA.

Westman, M., & Eden, D. (1997). Effects of a respite from work on burnout: Vacation relief and fade-out. *Journal of Applied Psychology, 82*, 516–527.

Westman, M., & Etzion, D. (2001). The impact of vacation and job stress on burnout and absenteeism. *Psychology and Health, 16*, 595–606.

Zijlstra, F. R. H. (1993). *Efficiency in work behaviour: A design approach for modern tools* (PhD thesis, Delft University of Technology). Delft, The Netherlands: Delft University Press.

Zijlstra, F. R. H., Roe, R., Leonova, A. B., & Krediet, I. (1999). Temporal factors in mental work: Effects of interrupted activities. *Journal of Occupational and Organizational Psychology, 72*, 163–186.

Zijlstra, F. R. H., Schalk, M. J. D., & Roe, R. A. (1996). Veranderingen in de Arbeid. Consequenties voor Werkenden [Changes in work: Consequences for working people]. *Tijdschrift voor Arbeidsvraagstukken, 12*, 251–263.

EUROPEAN JOURNAL OF WORK AND
ORGANIZATIONAL PSYCHOLOGY
2006, 15 (2), 139–157

Recovery opportunities, work – home interference, and well-being among managers

Toon W. Taris and Debby G. J. Beckers

*Department of Work and Organizational Psychology, Radboud University
Nijmegen, Nijmegen, The Netherlands*

Lotus C. Verhoeven

*Department of Social Psychology, Vrije Universiteit Amsterdam, Amsterdam,
The Netherlands*

Sabine A. E. Geurts, Michiel A. J. Kompier, and
Dimitri van der Linden

*Department of Work and Organizational Psychology, Radboud University
Nijmegen, Nijmegen, The Netherlands*

The present study addressed the associations among various indicators of
effort expenditure at work and recovery opportunities (perceived job demands
and job control, hours worked overtime, hours worked according to one's
contract), work – home interference, and well-being (exhaustion and
enjoyment) in a cross-sectional study among 117 male and 82 female
managers. Drawing on effort-recovery theory, we expected that high job
demands, low job control, a high number of hours worked overtime, and a
full-time appointment would be associated with high levels of work – home
interference, low levels of enjoyment, and high levels of exhaustion. Stepwise
regression analysis largely supported the hypothesis that high job demands and
low job control are associated with adverse work outcomes. However, the
effects of the number of hours worked overtime and according to one's
contract were usually weak and insignificant, suggesting that high effort
expenditure does not necessarily have adverse health consequences.

Research in the area of occupational health psychology has frequently
demonstrated that workers who expend much effort to their work may come

Correspondence should be addressed to Dr. T. W. Taris, Radboud University Nijmegen,
Department of Work and Organizational Psychology, PO Box 9104, NL-6500 HE Nijmegen,
The Netherlands. E-mail: t.taris@psych.ru.nl

http://www.psypress.com/ejwop   DOI: 10.1080/13594320500513889

to experience serious health problems in time (e.g., De Croon, Sluiter, & Frings-Dresen, 2003; Van Amelsfoort, Kant, Bültmann, & Swaen, 2003; Van der Hulst, 2003). Theoretically, these outcomes can be understood as the result of a chronic imbalance between the effort invested in the job and one's recovery opportunities, both during the working day (internal recovery, e.g., by alternating strenuous tasks with tasks that require less effort or by taking a break) and outside working hours (external recovery) (Meijman & Mulder, 1998; Sonnentag, 2001; Van der Hulst & Geurts, 2001).

There are several reasons why workers may not fully recover from their efforts. *Internal* recovery may be impeded by the presence of high job demands and low job control. High-demand jobs offer their incumbents little opportunity to recover from their efforts during the working day, because there will always be another deadline approaching that makes it necessary to keep working at full tilt. Lack of control implies that workers cannot align their work tasks with their current need for recovery, restricting their possibilities for internal recovery (cf. Karasek & Theorell, 1990) According to Merllié and Paoli (2001), 29% of European workers have no say about the pace of their work; 39% cannot decide when to take a break; 56% work at high speed; and 60% work to tight deadlines. These figures suggest that many jobs provide little opportunity for internal recovery. *External* recovery is inhibited by the degree to which workers must work longer hours than formally required. As they will recover from their work efforts during their off-work time, working overtime by definition reduces one's opportunities to recover from work. According to Merllié and Paoli, 20% of the European employees work on average more than 44 hours a week. This figure is even higher for managers (the target group in the present study), who work on average about 50 hours a week (Brett & Stroh, 2003; Lyon & Woodward, 2004).

Given the high percentages of employees working overtime and/or reporting high job demands, it is not surprising that research on the antecedents of *work – home interference* (WHI, defined in terms of the degree to which work demands clash with adequate and pleasurable performance in nonwork roles) has flourished over the past decade (Eby, Casper, Lockwood, Bordeaux, & Brinkley, 2005; Geurts & Demerouti, 2003, for overviews). In the present study we construe WHI as the result of adverse job conditions that constrain the opportunities for internal and external recovery. Although current evidence on the relationships among indicators of (lack of) recovery, WHI and worker well-being seems fairly consistent (high effort expenditure and lack of recovery are associated with high levels of WHI and low levels of well-being, e.g., De Croon et al., 2003; Eby et al., 2005; Geurts, Kompier, Roxburgh, & Houtman, 2003; Grzywacz & Marks, 2000; but see Beckers et al., 2004, and Gareis & Barnett, 2002, for null findings), several issues have remained unresolved. One of these is that most research on the effects of recovery on worker well-being has focused on the effects of lack of recovery on stress, strain and ill-health (e.g., sickness absence, De Croon et al., 2003, Sluiter, De Croon, Meijman, & Frings-Dresen, 2003; exhaustion, Geurts et al., 2003; psychological distress, Gareis & Barnett, 2002; or psychosomatic complaints, Bakker & Geurts, 2004; Sluiter, Frings-Dresen, Van der Beek, & Meijman, 2001, and Sonnentag, 2003, for notable exceptions). However, the concept of worker well-being would seem much broader, also encompassing positive dimensions such as motivation and satisfaction (Van Horn, Taris, Schaufeli, & Schreurs, 2004). By including both negative (exhaustion, work–home interference) and positive (work enjoyment) indicators of worker well-being, we explore whether the effects of effort expenditure and lack of recovery are similar for different facets of well-being.

A second unresolved issue is that, in examining the effects of long working hours (as an indicator of effort expenditure) on WHI and worker well-being, previous research did not usually distinguish between the effects of the number of overtime hours and the number of hours worked according to one's contract. Instead, researchers tended to focus on concepts such as the *total* number of hours spent in work (e.g., Barnett, Gareis, & Brennan, 1999; Sluiter, Van der Beek, & Frings-Dresen, 1999; Sonnentag, 2001). However, the effects of working overtime (as an occasionally occurring, unplanned, and short-notice form of effort expenditure) may well differ from those of the number of hours specified in one's contract. Whereas overtime draws on time that was initially and structurally reserved for external recovery or obligations in the nonwork domain, the number of hours specified in one's contract refers to time that had already been structurally allocated to effort expenditure and not to recovery or nonwork obligations.

In the present study we ask whether the effects of indicators of effort expenditure and internal versus external recovery opportunities relate in a similar fashion to positive and negative indicators of worker well-being. We also ask whether the effects of working overtime differ from those of the number of hours worked according to one's contract. These two issues are addressed in a cross-sectional study among 199 staff members of a large Dutch retail organization. Below we discuss the theoretical background of the study in more detail.

THE EFFORT-RECOVERY MODEL

The Effort-Recovery (E-R) model (Meijman & Mulder, 1998) is a work psychological model that is rooted in exercise physiology, and particularly in its application to the study of workload in relation to a person's capacity. The E-R model presumes that *effort expenditure* (i.e., work) is associated with short-term physiological and psychological costs. Normally these costs are reversible: After a shorter or longer break from work and the accompanying effort investments, psychobiological systems will restabilize to a baseline level (*recovery*). High workload will thus not have negative consequences, as long as the possibilities for recovery during and after the working day are sufficient.

However, workers may have insufficient opportunities for internal and external recovery from work. High job demands may necessitate high effort expenditure during the work day, simultaneously restricting the possibilities for internal recovery—no time to take a break. Likewise, effort expenditure may continue after one's working time is formally over, e.g., when workers are forced to work overtime because they have too little time to complete all their work tasks during the standard working day, or because negative load effects built up at work do not unfold immediately after respite from work but last during evening hours (e.g., when workers experience difficulty relaxing) due to a slow process of unwinding (Geurts et al., 2003; Sluiter et al., 2001; Sonnentag, 2001). In such cases a downwards spiral may be activated. Workers, not yet fully recovered from the previous work day, must invest additional (compensatory) effort to perform adequately during the next working period, resulting in an increased intensity of negative load reactions that appeal even stronger to the recovery process. Continuous or frequent exposure to high workload in combination with insufficient recovery may thus lead to an accumulation of negative load effects that may persist for a longer period of time (e.g., exhaustion, psychosomatic complaints, and lack of work engagement), eventually becoming irreversible and manifest (De Croon et al., 2003).

EFFORT EXPENDITURE AND OPPORTUNITIES FOR RECOVERY

As argued earlier, the opportunities for *internal* recovery primarily depend on the characteristics of one's work. Research based on Karasek and Theorell's (1990) Demand–Control model has shown that high job demands and low levels of job control are associated with high levels of strain and mental and physical complaints (De Lange, Taris, Kompier, Houtman, & Bongers, 2003; Van der Doef & Maes, 1999, for reviews), and low levels of positive outcomes such as learning and satisfaction (Taris & Kompier, 2005, for a review). In the context of the E-R model, incumbents of high demand jobs must expend much effort, possibly—due to their high work load—without having the opportunity to take an occasional break (i.e., low opportunities for internal recovery). Job control concerns the amount of say workers have over their work, the methods they apply, and the order in which they handle their tasks (Karasek & Theorell, 1990). In particular, the last-mentioned aspect, job control, seems relevant here;

workers who can decide about the order in which they carry out their tasks are able to alternate their tasks, such that they maximize their opportunities for recovery. Thus, both low job control and high job demands can be linked to the absence of opportunities for internal recovery (Sluiter et al., 2003). Based on these notions, we expect that employees reporting high job demands (representing high effort expenditure and low opportunities for recovery during the working day) will experience high levels of exhaustion (Hypothesis 1a), low levels of enjoyment (Hypothesis 1b), and high levels of work – home interference (Hypothesis 1c). Further, high levels of job control were expected to be associated with high levels of exhaustion (Hypothesis 2a), low levels of enjoyment (Hypothesis 2b), and high levels of work – home interference (Hypothesis 2c).

The opportunities for *external* recovery have been associated with the number of hours spent on the job. Many studies report adverse effects of working long hours on worker health and well-being (Van der Hulst, 2003). In the E-R model, this result is interpreted by assuming that working long hours both increases effort expenditure and reduces the time available for unwinding and recovery (e.g., Jansen, Kant, Van Amelsvoort, Nijhuis, & Van den Brandt, 2003; Sonnentag, 2001). Interestingly, researchers usually do not distinguish between the effects of long working days and those of working overtime (e.g., Sluiter et al., 2003; Sonnentag, 2001). Obviously, the total number of working hours is the sum of the (fixed) number of hours a worker must spend working according to one's contract, and the (variable) number of hours spent working overtime.

Number of hours worked according to one's contract

When workers decide on the number of hours they structurally spend on work (that is, the number of hours specified in their contract), they will often take into consideration that they will need a certain amount of time for other activities (e.g., domestic obligations, leisure activities) and that they must generate a particular income to sustain their way of life. Thus, within organizational constraints, any choice for working a particular number of hours is the result of a more or less conscious process of deliberation about the pros and cons of working some hours extra or a couple of hours less. As workers will strive towards a good fit between their work schedule, their own needs and those of their partners, children, and other dependants (*schedule fit*, cf. Barnett, 1998; Eby et al., 2005; Gareis & Barnett, 2002), workers taking on a particular (part- or full-time) appointment will have good reasons for doing so: The number of hours specified in their work contract will be geared towards their anticipated nonwork obligations and their preferences regarding the balance between work and other activities.

This reasoning suggests that the number of hours worked according to one's contract should not be a major predictor of work–home interference. Interestingly, previous research on the effects of long working hours has not unequivocally supported the idea that long working hours are related to high work–home interference and adverse work outcomes. Whereas Eby et al. (2005) conclude that "conflict is higher among those who work a greater number of hours or longer days" (p. 143), Barnett (1998) argues that "the assumption that long work hours inevitably give rise to work/family conflict and negative personal outcomes is strongly challenged" (p. 132). The apparent discrepancy between these conclusions (which were both based on extensive literature reviews) might be due to the fact that previous research has confounded the effects of having part-time versus full-time employment and those of the number of hours worked overtime. In the absence of evidence pertaining to the distinction between these two concepts, we expect employees who work a high number of hours according to their contracts to report high levels of exhaustion (Hypothesis 3a), low levels of enjoyment (Hypothesis 3b), and high levels of work–home interference (Hypothesis 3c).

Number of hours worked overtime

Every now and then there may be more work to be done than is possible within the boundaries of one's formal appointment. If so, workers will consider whether they can and are willing to spend extra time to their work. However, the decision to work overtime differs from the decision regarding taking on full- or part-time employment in that (a) the occurrence of the need to work overtime may be hard to predict, making it difficult to align these extra work tasks with one's regular nonwork tasks, the time needed for recovery, and one's own needs and those of others (e.g., one's spouse and children); and (b) working overtime draws on time resources that were initially (i.e., when deciding about the full- or part-time employment) reserved for recovery from the regular working day or for nonwork obligations. Thus, working overtime should have stronger consequences for workers' opportunities for external recovery than the plain number of hours specified in one's labour contract as the latter involves a structural long-term obligation that will usually be firmly imbedded in one's daily (or, perhaps, weekly) routine. This can be linked to earlier discussions of the role of schedule fit (Barnett et al., 1999; Gareis & Barnett, 2002), in that working overtime (being an essentially unpredictable phenomenon) makes it more difficult to realize an acceptable equilibrium between one's work schedule and the needs of oneself and one's dependants than simply working many hours according to one's contract (being a fixed and predictable phenomenon). Thus, employees who work a high number of hours of overtime will report high levels of exhaustion (Hypothesis 4a), low levels of enjoyment (Hypothesis 4b), and high levels of work–home interference (Hypothesis 4c).

METHOD

Sample

This study features a sample of higher level staff of the head office of a Dutch retail organization with 50,000 employees. All females and half of the males in the six highest salary scales (starting at 45,000 euros a year gross) received a questionnaire addressing background variables, work character-istics, subjective well-being, work–home interference, and overtime. After three weeks 199 completed questionnaires had been returned, yielding a 48.5% response rate (58.8% male; M_{age} 39.6 years, $SD = 8.3$; 90.4% held at least a college degree; the average number of years in their present job was 3.0 years, $SD = 3.6$; 96.5% of the sample supervised on average 6.3 others, $SD = 24.4$; 6.0% of the sample had a contract for less than 32 hours a week, 20.7% for 32–38 hours a week, and 73.4% for 40 hours a week). Although the participants could compensate for their overtime by taking time off in lieu, on average they worked 8.0 hours extra per week ($SD = 5.6$). Further, 92% of the participants lived with a partner (either married or unmarried) who usually (71%) had a paid job as well, and 49% of the participants had young children (<6 years old).

Variables

Exhaustion.   This was measured using the 5-item exhaustion scale of the Maslach Burnout Inventory—General Survey (MBI-GS; Schaufeli, Leiter, Maslach, & Jackson, 1996). A typical item is "I feel used up at the end of the work day" (0 = "never", 6 = "every day"), alpha = .83. High scores reflect high levels of exhaustion.

Enjoyment.   This was measured using the 7-item enjoyment scale devised by Spence and Robbins (1992). A typical item is "Most of the time my work is very pleasurable" (1 = strongly disagree", 5 = "strongly agree", alpha = .67). High scores indicate high levels of enjoyment.

Work–home interference.   This was measured with six items, four of which were derived from the Survey Work–Home Interaction Nijmegen (SWING; Geurts et al., 2005). Following current theorizing (Greenhaus & Beutell, 1985), we distinguished between *strain-based* interference (i.e., work strain "spills over" to the home domain, hampering the unwinding process), and *time-based* interference (i.e., time demands at work make it physically impossible to perform home obligations). Two items from the SWING represented strain-based negative work–home interference ("How often does it happen that you are irritable at home because your work is demanding?", and "How often does it happen that your work obligations make it difficult for you to feel relaxed at home?"). A third item was added: "How often does it happen that you do not fully enjoy the company of your spouse/family/friends because you worry about your work?" (1 = "never", 4 = "always", alpha = .79). Two other SWING items represented time-based work–home interference ("How often does it happen that you have to work so hard that you do not have time for any of your hobbies?", "How often does it happen that your work takes up time that you would have liked to spend with your spouse/family/friends?"). A third item was self-developed: "How often does it happen that you spend so much time working that you do not have time for things that personally matter to you", 1 = "never", 4 = "always", alpha = .81). High scores represent high levels of WHI.

Perceived quantitative job demands. These were measured using Karasek's (1985) 4-item scale, including items such as "My job requires that I work very fast", 1 = "never", 4 = "always", alpha = .83; high scores denote high job demands. *Perceived job control* was measured using Karasek's (1985) 3-item decision latitude scale, which includes items such as "Can you decide for yourself how you carry out your tasks?" (1 = "never", 4 = "always", alpha = .84; high scores signify high levels of control). *The average number of hours worked overtime* per week was measured by subtracting the number of hours per week the participants had to work according to their contract from the number of hours they said they worked on average per week. Finally, we included measures of the *number of hours the participants had to work according to their contract*, participant *gender, age, salary* (a 6-category proxy of job level), a variable indicating whether the participant had *young children* (< 6 years old), and the number of years of *experience in the present job* (ranging from 0 to 23 years). Table 1 presents the correlations among the variables, as well as their means and standard deviations.

Statistical analysis

Distinction among the outcome variables. Table 1 reveals that three of the four outcome variables employed in this study (time-based and strain-based WHI, and exhaustion) correlate substantially, rs vary from .52 to .62, all $ps < .001$. This makes it desirable to verify whether concepts can be

TABLE 1
Means, standard deviations, and correlations for the study variables ($N = 199$)

Variables	1	2	3	4	5	6	7	8	9	10	11	12	13
1 Exhaustion	1.00												
2 Enjoyment	-.35	1.00											
3 Time-based WHI	.52	-.14	1.00										
4 Strain-based WHI	.59	-.21	.62	1.00									
5 No. hours overtime	.03	.13	.31	.23	1.00								
6 Perceived job demands	.33	-.11	.56	.42	.35	1.00							
7 Perceived job control	-.22	.23	-.08	-.15	.17	-.04	1.00						
8 No. hours contract	-.06	.05	-.02	-.01	.32	.06	.01	1.00					
9 Gender[a]	.01	.02	.01	-.02	-.21	.00	-.08	-.44	1.00				
10 Age	.08	-.12	-.06	.01	-.03	.05	-.17	-.04	.38	1.00			
11 Salary	-.07	.08	.22	.12	.33	.14	.28	.02	-.13	-.27	1.00		
12 Young children present[b]	-.18	.16	.02	.02	-.07	-.09	.26	-.16	.36	-.36	.24	1.00	
13 Experience	.04	-.02	.09	.10	.07	.08	-.04	-.01	-.13	-.41	.02	.17	1.00
M	1.41	3.48	1.91	1.90	7.98	2.60	3.12	37.90	1.41	39.61	2.76	0.49	2.97
SD	1.11	0.81	0.59	0.50	5.63	0.56	0.44	4.08	0.49	8.33	1.49	0.39	3.63

Correlations of .14 and over are significant at $p < .05$.

[a] 0 = male, 1 = female.

[b] 0 = has no young children (<6 years old), 1 = has young children.

147

distinguished empirically. To this aim, a series of preliminary confirmatory factor analyses (CFA; Jöreskog & Sörbom, 1999) was carried out in which several models for the relations among the items of these three scales were compared. The first model (M_1) was a model in which all 11 items of the three respective scales loaded on one underlying dimension. The second model (M_2) involved three factors, with the three items tapping strain-based work–home interference loading on the first dimension, the three items measuring time-based work–home interference on the second dimension, and the five exhaustion items loading on the third dimension. The three dimensions in this model were allowed to correlate. Model fit was assessed using the standard chi-square test, as well as the root mean squared residual (RMSEA), the non-normed fit index (NNFI), and the comparative fit index (CFI). Values of .10 and lower for RMSEA, and of .90 and over for NNFI and CFI indicate acceptable model fit (Byrne, 2001).

Whereas M_1 fitted the data badly, chi-square ($N = 199$, $df = 44) = 209.2$, RMSEA $= .16$, NNFI $= .79$, CFI $= .83$, the three-factor model M_2 fitted the data significantly better, chi-square ($N = 199$, $df = 41) = 60.1$, RMSEA $= .05$, NNFI $= .97$, CFI $= .98$, chi-square ($M_1 - M_2) = 149.1$ with 3 df, $p < .001$. Further, three additional two-factor models were tested in which the items of two of the three underlying scales loaded on one dimension (e.g., all six WHI items), and the items of the third underlying scale on the second dimension (e.g., all five exhaustion items). The three-factor model fitted the data significantly better than these three two-factor models ($p < .01$ for all three chi-square difference tests; results not reported here for the sake of brevity). Taken together, these results demonstrate that exhaustion, strain-based, and time-based WHI can be distinguished empirically.

Regression analyses.   Hypotheses 1a–4c on the relations among well-being (enjoyment and exhaustion) and strain-based and time-based WHI on the one hand, and the opportunities for internal recovery (i.e., perceived demands and control) and external recovery (the number of hours worked according to one's contract and the number of hours worked overtime) on the other, were tested in a series of four stepwise regression analyses, one for each outcome variable. In the first step we entered participant age, gender, presence vs. absence of young children, number of years of experience in the present job, and salary level. In the second step we added the effects of perceived job demands, perceived job control, number of hours of overtime worked, and the number of hours worked according to one's contract. In several preliminary analyses, we examined whether addition of the nonlinear effects of demands, control, number of hours worked overtime, and the number of hours worked according to one's contract contributed significantly to the explanation of the outcome variables. These nonlinear effects were not significant, however. Similarly, we tested whether the Demand × Control and Number of hours worked overtime × Number of hours worked according to one's contract interactions explained additional variance in the outcome variables. Again, these effects were not significant. Consequently, in the remainder we focus on main effects only.

RESULTS

Table 2 presents the standardized least squares estimates of our four regression analyses for recovery opportunities, WHI, and employee well-being. The explanatory variables accounted for 21% of the variance in *exhaustion*, $p < .001$. Employees perceiving high job demands reported higher levels of exhaustion than others (a standardized effect of $-.34$, $p < .001$; Hypothesis 1a was supported). Contrary to our expectations, employees holding a full-time appointment, employees who reported high levels of overtime, or those who reported low levels of job control were *not* more likely to experience higher levels of exhaustion than others (Hypotheses 2a, 3a, and 4a were rejected). Indeed, employees with a full-time appointment reported lower levels of exhaustion than others (an effect of $-.17$, $p < .05$; note that the corresponding correlation coefficient was only $-.06$, *ns*, cf. Table 1).

As regards *enjoyment*, the explanatory variables accounted for 14% of the variance in enjoyment, $p < .01$. As expected, low perceived job demands and high perceived control were associated with high levels of enjoyment, although these effects were weak (effects of $-.16$ and $.15$, *ps* $< .05$, respectively; Hypotheses 1b and 2b were supported). Further, whereas there was no significant association between contract hours and enjoyment (Hypothesis 3b was rejected), we found a positive association between the number of hours worked overtime and enjoyment—employees who spend much time working overtime seem to enjoy their work more, rather than less than others (an effect of $.21$, $p < .05$; Hypothesis 4b was rejected—note that the correlation that underlies this effect was $.13$, *ns*).

With respect to *strain-based* and *time-based work–home interference*, we found that perceived high job demands and low job control were associated with high levels of interference (standardized effects of $.34$ and $-.20$, *ps* < 01, for strain-based WHI, and $.48$ and $-.15$, *ps* $< .05$, for time-based WHI, respectively; Hypotheses 1c/2c were supported). There was no association between the number of hours worked according to one's contract and either type of work–home interference (Hypothesis 3c was rejected), but high levels of overtime were associated with high levels of time-based WHI (an effect of $.16$, $p < .05$; Hypothesis 4c was partially supported).

TABLE 2

Results of four stepwise regression analyses on exhaustion, enjoyment, and two forms of work–home interference (standardized least squares estimates)

	Exhaustion		Enjoyment		Strain-based WHI		Time-based WHI	
	Step 1	Step 2	Step 1	Step 2	Step 1	Step 2	Step 1	Step 2
Age	.09	.06	−.15	−.17	.07	.00	−.03	−.12
Salary	−.02	−.03	.04	−.05	.11	.05	.22**	.10
Gender[a]	−.07	−.16	.12	.24*	−.04	−.04	.04	.07
Young children present[b]	−.19*	−.19*	.14	.19*	.02	−.06	.05	−.06
Experience	.12	.07	−.10	−.10	.13	.06	.09	.00
No. hours contract		−.17*		.13		−.09		−.07
Overtime		−.05		.21*		.12		.16*
Perceived job demands		.34***		−.16*		.34***		.48***
Perceived job control		−.14		.15*		−.20**		−.15*
R^2	.05	.21***	.05	.14**	.04	.22***	.07*	.37***
R^2 change		.15***		.09**		.18***		.30***

*$p < .05$, **$p < .01$, ***$p < .001$.
[a] 0 = male, 1 = female.
[b] 0 = has no young children (<6 years old), 1 = has young children.

DISCUSSION

The present study was intended to shed more light on (a) whether the effects of working overtime differ from those of the number of hours worked according to one's contract, and (b) the degree to which the effects of the opportunities for internal and external recovery are similar for negative and positive work outcomes.

Overtime and contract hours

Whereas high perceived demands were consistently and sometimes strongly associated with lower well-being (i.e., low levels of enjoyment, and high levels of work – home interference and exhaustion), the results obtained for the number of hours worked overtime and the number of hours worked according to one's contract provided all but strong evidence for the idea that employees who spend much time to work have few opportunities for external recovery. Although overtime and contract hours were indeed differentially related to exhaustion and enjoyment, their effects were weak and often not in accordance with our expectations. For example, we found that participants who worked full-time reported relatively low, rather than high, levels of exhaustion, whereas participants who spent many hours on overwork (i.e., work outside contracted hours) reported relatively high, rather than low, levels of enjoyment. In this light, it is interesting to note that previous research also reported similar reversed associations between effort expenditure and work outcomes. For example, Beckers et al. (2004) found that overworkers were generally nonfatigued, motivated workers, which meshes well with the findings summarized in Barnett (1998).

One interpretation of these theoretically somewhat anomalous effects is that effort investment is rewarding; e.g., it could lead to all sorts of (material and immaterial) benefits, and these could outweigh this extra effort expenditure (note that Brett & Stroh, 2003, found no support for this reasoning). However, it is also possible that in these instances we are dealing with two cases of mistaken causality. Workers for whom a full-time appointment is too demanding may in time take on a part-time appointment, because they come to realize that they cannot combine a full-time appointment with their nonwork obligations and opportunities for recovery (e.g., Taris, 1997). Similarly, enthusiastic workers who truly enjoy their jobs may well have fewer objections to working overtime than others— if your job gives you pleasure, spending more time on it than is actually necessary may not be such a bad thing (cf. Van der Hulst & Geurts, 2001). Thus, it would seem possible that the effort expended to work not only affects worker motivation and health, but that the latter two variables affect effort expenditure as well. Due to its cross-sectional study design, the present study cannot unambiguously unravel the causal direction of the associations among overtime, contract hours, exhaustion, and enjoyment. Together with Barnett (1998) we conclude, however, that there are no simple and easy-to-interpret relationships among these concepts; it is certainly not the case that working overtime and/or full-time always has adverse effects on worker well-being.

Further, we found that the *number of hours worked overtime* was positively associated with time-based WHI. Consistent with Meijman and Mulder's (1998) Effort-Recovery framework, this suggests that when workers work longer hours than is formally required, this interferes with the time needed for their nonwork tasks. Note that there is no corresponding effect of overtime on strain-based WHI, suggesting that as a rule working overtime does not result in work strain spilling over to the home domain.

Differences between positive and negative work outcomes

Our second question was whether the effects of recovery differ for positive (enjoyment) and negative (exhaustion) outcomes. We found few differences between the patterns of results for these two types of variables. The proportions of explained variance were quite low for both exhaustion and enjoyment; although the study variables explained more variance in exhaustion (21%) than in enjoyment (14%), this difference was largely due to a relatively strong effect of perceived job demands on exhaustion. As earlier research has abundantly shown that workers who report that they work hard also tend to indicate that they are exhausted (De Lange et al., 2003; Van der Doef & Maes, 1999), this finding is hardly surprising. More interesting is that enjoyment was related to the number of hours worked overtime. This indicates that employees who enjoy their work tend to work longer hours. Further, exhausted workers were slightly more often working part-time, suggesting that workers who structurally spend too much time to work in relation to their other obligations tend to reduce their effort expenditure to work (Taris, 1997). These notions suggest that it may be worthwhile to examine the relations between effort expenditure, worker health, and work motivation longitudinally, focusing not only on the effects of effort expenditure on health and well-being, but also on reverse relationships (e.g., De Lange, Taris, Kompier, Houtman, & Bongers, 2005).

Study limitations

Several limitations of this study are worth noting. First, the data were collected using a cross-sectional design, meaning that no conclusions regarding the causal direction of effects can be drawn. This limitation is important, because at least two unexpected results (i.e., the finding that overtime was positively, rather than negatively, associated with enjoyment; and the finding that the number of hours worked according to one's contract was negatively, rather than positively, related to exhaustion) may be interpreted as cases of mistaken causal dominance. The positive association between the number of hours worked overtime and enjoyment can be interpreted by assuming that workers who enjoy their work will be more motivated to work a couple of hours extra than those who do not (cf. Beckers et al., 2004). Similarly, it would seem plausible that workers experience high levels of fatigue due to their job will reduce the number of hours they spend to work (which may be considered a form of active coping behaviour). Both interpretations question the common assumption that spending much time to work (in the form of working overtime, working long hours, or working full-time as opposed to part-time) necessarily leads to adverse work outcomes. Thorough examination of these theoretically interesting notions requires a repeated-measures design.

Second, as all the data in this study were self-report, common method variance and negative affectivity may have biased our findings. To assess the impact of these problems, two tests described in Podsakoff, MacKenzie, Lee, and Podsakoff (2003) were conducted (details on these can be obtained from the first author). Harman one-factor tests indicated that the four criterion variables and the measures of demands, control, and overtime could empirically be distinguished from each other, suggesting that common method variance or negative affectivity were not expected contaminants of the structural results. Further, confirmatory factor analyses revealed that common method variance accounted for only 4.2% of the covariance among the items. Thus, while there are effects of common method variance/negative affectivity in this study, the bias resulting thereof is relatively small.

A third issue is whether the number of hours worked is a good indicator of effort expenditure. Working long hours is not necessarily exhausting; this depends on the level and type of activity required during these work hours as well. As the present sample consists of higher staff recruited from the six highest salary brackets in a large profit organization operating in an extremely competitive environment, it seems reasonable to assume that our participants bear much responsibility and take relatively complex decisions that involve much information processing, and that may severely impact the organization and its employees. Thus, it would seem likely that our managers not only spend much time at work, but also that they expend much effort during these working hours.

A fourth issue derives from the nature of the present sample in combination with our conceptualization of overwork as something that occurs irregularly and largely unpredictably, thus interfering more strongly with nonwork obligations and leisure activities than structural work obligations. However, for the current sample of highly paid professionals, overtime may be a regularly occurring phenomenon that is firmly embedded in one's daily routine and will thus not interfere heavily with nonwork activities and opportunities for recovery. Of the present sample, no fewer than 64% worked on average at least 44 hours a week. Thus, for a considerable proportion of our participants working overtime seems "business as usual", meaning that the effects of overtime on WHI and worker well-being may have been estimated conservatively due to restriction-of-range effects.

A fifth point concerns the issue of whether the joint effect of the number of hours worked overtime and the number of hours worked according to one's contract may be stronger than their main effects only. To examine this issue, we tested whether addition of the statistical interaction between number of hours worked overtime and number of hours worked according to one's contract accounted for additional variance in the outcome variables, after controlling for the main effects of these variables. This interaction was insignificant for all four outcome variables, meaning that the total number of hours worked was not a substantially better predictor of these outcomes than its two constituent variables.

Study implications

In spite of these limitations, we believe that our results hold implications for both theory and practice. Scientifically, one important issue that should be addressed in future research concerns the relationship between work motivation, the number of hours spent at work and worker health. The results presented here suggest that these relationships cannot be construed as resulting from a simple one-directional process in which effort expenditure (spending much time at work) and a corresponding lack of recovery (working long hours means that less time for recovery is left) *automatically* and *necessarily* result in ill-health and lack of motivation. It would seem to make sense to examine these relationships as the possible product of a reciprocal self-regulatory process in which high effort expenditure and lack of recovery result in low well-being, whereas lower well-being may result in lower effort expenditure. It might be speculated that in the long run both processes will lead to a situation in which levels of effort expenditure, recovery opportunities, work motivation, and well-being will reach stable states that are optimally aligned with each other—an equilibrium that will only incidentally be disturbed by outside forces (e.g., unfavourable changes in one's tasks or the work context, or similar changes in the family context).

Our results also provide some evidence regarding our distinction between the number of hours worked overtime versus the number of hours worked according to one's contract. Both concepts showed different patterns of relationships to the other variables included in the present study, supporting our assumption that it is not only how many hours people spend on work, but also the degree to which their work obligations interfere with nonwork activities that determine whether they will experience adverse consequences for well-being (cf. Van der Hulst & Geurts, 2001).

Practically, perhaps the most noteworthy feature of the present study is the finding that long working hours do not necessarily have severe and adverse consequences for health and well-being; the associations between the number of hours worked overtime, the number of hours worked according to one's contract, and the outcome variables were generally weak and insignificant, and sometimes in the opposite direction. Although these associations may have been underestimated in the present study due to the homogeneity of the sample, our findings show that for at least *some* types of workers in *some* contexts, high effort expenditure (i.e., long working hours) and the correspondingly low opportunities for recovery do not affect their health and well-being negatively. The question remains *why* this is so. E-R theory suggests that these workers may have minimized their nonwork obligations, meaning that they have sufficient opportunities to recover from their work efforts. Alternatively, working hard may yield favourable outcomes (e.g., high earnings, prestige, promotion opportunities, satisfaction) that could compensate high effort expenditure (Brett & Stroh, 2003). The present study does not allow for examining these explanations; follow-up research is needed to generate more insight in these intriguing notions.

REFERENCES

Bakker, A., & Geurts, S. A. E. (2004). Towards a dual-process model of work–home interference. *Work and Occupations, 31*, 345–366.

Barnett, R. C. (1998). Towards a review and reconceptualization of the work/family literature. *Genetic, Social, and General Psychology Monographs, 124*, 125–182.

Barnett, R. C., Gareis, K. C., & Brennan, R. T. (1999). Fit as a mediator of the relationship between work hours and burnout. *Journal of Occupational Health Psychology, 4*, 307–317.

Beckers, D. G. J., van der Linden, D., Smulders, P. G. W., Kompier, M. A. J., van Veldhoven, M. J. P. M., & van Yperen, N. W. (2004). Working overtime hours: Relations with fatigue, work motivation, and the quality of work. *Journal of Occupational and Environmental Medicine, 46*, 1282–1289.

Brett, J. M., & Stroh, L. K. (2003). Working 61 plus hours a week: Why do managers do it? *Journal of Applied Psychology, 88*, 67–78.

Byrne, B. M. (2001). *Structural equation modeling with AMOS: Basic concepts, applications, and programming.* Mahwah, NJ: Lawrence Erlbaum Associates, Inc.

De Croon, E. M., Sluiter, J. K., & Frings-Dresen, M. H. W. (2003). Need for recovery after work predicts sickness absence: A 2-year prospective cohort study in truck drivers. *Journal of Psychosomatic Research, 55*, 331–339.

De Lange, A. H., Taris, T. W., Kompier, M. A. J., Houtman, I. L. D., & Bongers, P. M. (2003). The *very* best of the millennium: Longitudinal research on the Job Demands–Control model. *Journal of Occupational Health Psychology, 8*, 282–305.

De Lange, A. J., Taris, T. W., Kompier, M. A. J., Houtman, I. L. D., & Bongers, P. M. (2005). Different mechanisms to explain the reversed effects of mental health on work characteristics. *Scandinavian Journal of Work, Environment, and Health, 31*, 3–14.

Eby, L. T., Casper, W. J., Lockwood, A., Bordeaux, C., & Brinkley, A. (2005). Work and family research in IO/OB: Content analysis and review of the literature (1980–2002). *Journal of Vocational Behavior, 66*, 124–197.

Gareis, K. C., & Barnett, R. C. (2002). Under what conditions do long work hours affect psychological distress? *Work and Occupations, 29*, 483–497.

Geurts, S. A. E., & Demerouti, E. (2003). The work–home interface: State-of-the-art and future research agenda. In M. Schabracq, J. Winnubst, & C. L. Cooper (Eds.), *Handbook of work and health psychology* (2nd ed.). Chichester, UK: Wiley.

Geurts, S. A. E., Kompier, M. A. J., Roxburgh, S., & Houtman, I. L. (2003). Does work–home interference mediate the relationship between workload and well-being? *Journal of Vocational Behavior, 63*, 532–559.

Geurts, S. A. E., Taris, T. W., Kompier, M. A. J., Dikkers, S. J. E., van Hooff, M., & Kinnunen, U. (2005). Work – home interaction from a work psychological perspective: Development and validation of a new questionnaire, the SWING. *Work & Stress, 19*, 319–339.

Greenhaus, J. H., & Beutell, N. J. (1985). Sources of conflict between work and family roles. *Academy of Management Review, 10*, 76–88.

Grzywacz, J. G., & Marks, N. F. (2000). Reconceptualizing the work–family interface: An ecological perspective on the correlates of positive and negative spillover between work and family. *Journal of Occupational Health Psychology, 5*, 111–126.

Jansen, N. W. H., Kant, I. J., Van Amelsvoort, L. G. P. M., Nijhuis, F. J. N., & Van den Brandt, P. A. (2003). Need for recovery from work: Evaluating short-term effects of working hours, patterns and schedules. *Ergonomics, 46*, 664–680.

Jöreskog, K. G., & Sörbom, D. (1999). *LISREL 8.30* [Software]. Chicago: Scientific Software.

Karasek, R. A. (1985). *Job Content Instrument: Questionnaire and user's guide.* Los Angeles: Department of Industrial and Systems Engineering, University of Southern California.

Karasek, R. A., & Theorell, T. (1990). *Healthy work: Stress, productivity, and the reconstruction of working life.* New York: Basic Books.

Lyon, D., & Woodward, A. E. (2004). Gender and time at the top. *European Journal of Women's Studies, 11*, 205–221.

Meijman, T. F., & Mulder, G. (1998). Psychological aspects of workload. In P. J. Drenth, H. Thierry, & C. J. de Wolff (Eds.), *Handbook of work and organizational psychology* (2nd ed., pp. 5–33). Hove, UK: Psychology Press.

Merllié, D., & Paoli, P. (2001). *Ten years of working conditions in the European Union.* Dublin, Ireland: European Foundation for the Improvement of Living and Working Conditions.

Podsakoff, P. M., MacKenzie, S. B., Lee, J. Y., & Podsakoff, N. P. (2003). Common method biases in behavioral research: A critical review of the literature and recommended remedies. *Journal of Applied Psychology, 88*, 879–903.

Schaufeli, W. B., Leiter, M. P., Maslach, C., & Jackson, S. E. (1996). Maslach Burnout Inventory—General Survey (MBI–GS). In C. Maslach, S. E. Jackson, & M. P. Leiter (Eds.), *MBI manual* (3rd ed.). Palo Alto, CA: Consulting Psychologists Press.

Sluiter, J. K., De Croon, E. M., Meijman, T. F., & Frings-Dresen, M. H. W. (2003). Need for recovery from work related fatigue and its role in the development and prediction of subjective health complaints. *Occupational and Environmental Medicine, 60*, i62–i70.

Sluiter, J. K., Frings-Dresen, M. H. W., Van der Beek, A. J., & Meijman, T. F. (2001). The relation between work-induced neuroendocrine reactivity and recovery, subjective need for recovery, and health status. *Journal of Psychosomatic Research, 50*, 29–37.

Sluiter, J. K., Van der Beek, A. J., & Frings-Dresen, M. H. W. (1999). The influence of work characteristics on the need for recovery and experienced health: A study on coach drivers. *Ergonomics, 42*, 573–583.

Sonnentag, S. (2001). Work, recovery activities, and individual well-being: A diary study. *Journal of Occupational Health Psychology, 6*, 196–210.

Sonnentag, S. (2003). Recovery, work engagement, and proactive behavior: A new look at the interface between nonwork and work. *Journal of Applied Psychology, 88*, 518–528.

Spence, J. T., & Robbins, A. S. (1992). Workaholism: Definition, measurement, and preliminary results. *Journal of Personality Assessment, 58*, 160–178.

Taris, T. W. (1997). Reconsidering the relations between female employment and fertility: Having children, full-time, and part-time employment. *International Journal of Sociology of the Family, 27*, 45–73.

Taris, T. W., & Kompier, M. A. J. (2005). Job characteristics and learning behavior. In P. L. Perrewé & D. C. Ganster (Eds.), *Research in occupational stress and well-being: Exploring interpersonal dynamics* (Vol. 4, pp. 127–166). Amsterdam: JAI Press.

Van Amelsfoort, L. G. P. M., Kant, I. J., Bültmann, U., & Swaen, G. M. H. (2003). Need for recovery after work and the subsequent risk of cardiovascular disease in a working population. *Occupational and Environmental Medicine, 60*, i83–i87.

Van der Doef, M. P., & Maes, S. (1999). The Job Demand–Control(–Support) Model and psychological well-being: A review of 20 years of empirical research. *Work and Stress, 13*, 87–114.

Van der Hulst, M. (2003). Long work hours and health. *Scandinavian Journal of Work, Environment, and Health, 29*, 171–188.

Van der Hulst, M., & Geurts, S. A. E. (2001). Associations between overtime and psychological health in high and low reward jobs. *Work and Stress, 15*, 227–240.

Van Horn, J. E., Taris, T. W., Schaufeli, W. B., & Schreurs, P. J. G. (2004). The structure of occupational well-being: A study among Dutch teachers. *Journal of Occupational and Organizational Psychology, 77*, 365–375.

EUROPEAN JOURNAL OF WORK AND
ORGANIZATIONAL PSYCHOLOGY
2006, 15 (2), 158–180

Learning opportunities at work as predictor for recovery and health

Renate Rau

University of Marburg, Marburg, Germany

One of the principles of good job design is to make jobs that are conducive to personal development and to health. One of the ways in which jobs can facilitate personal development is to provide learning opportunities. Therefore, this study tested the hypothesis that learning opportunities at work are positively related to health. The jobs of 185 men and women were evaluated and assessed for the learning opportunities provided by these jobs. Health was measured (a) as allostasis, operationalized as the body's ability to recover after load, and (b) as self-reports about mental health and life satisfaction. Objective indicators of allostasis were reduction of nocturnal heart rate and reduction of blood pressure after load. Subjective indicators were the ability to recover and absence of sleep disturbances. Linear and logistic regression analyses showed that learning opportunities were significantly related to a healthy cardiovascular behaviour with a strong reduction of nocturnal heart rate and blood pressure after a working day (allostasis). However, learning opportunities were only related to the objectively measured health variables, but not to self-reported data of health. The study findings suggest that designing jobs which provide learning opportunities is very important for workers' health. Thus job design can improve both personal development and health.

The aim of job design is to increase the efficiency and productivity of human work as well as to avoid occupational illness, accidents, and strain. One of the key principles of Action Theory (Hacker, 1986, 1993) is that job design should aim at facilitating peoples' actions, and that this will result in improved efficiency and good health of employees and opportunities for personal development (Hacker, 1993; Richter, 2000; Ulich, 2001; Volpert, Oesterreich, Gablenz Kolakovic, Krogoll, & Resch, 1983). However, what is meant by personal development has not yet been clearly defined in the

Correspondence should be addressed to Renate Rau, University of Marburg, Department of Psychology, Work and Organizational Psychology Unit, Gutenberg-Strasse 18, 35032 Marburg, Germany. E-mail: rau-ao@staff.uni-marburg.de

DOI: 10.1080/13594320500513905

literature. Thus, a range of different opportunities for personal development are provided during the process of work, each of which may refer to different aspects of the employees' personal characteristics. For example, through activities at work the job incumbent may develop his/her social, emotional, or cognitive competencies, motivation, skills, knowledge, etc., and even his/her self-concept (Ulich, 2001). It is preferable to avoid using the term "personal development" without specifying which aspects of personal development are referred to. Furthermore, also the particular job characteristics that are to be assessed in relation to those specific aspects of personal development should be specified.

As a specific example of the aim to design jobs that facilitate personal development (Hacker, 1993; Ulich, 2001; Volpert et al., 1983) one could think of designing jobs that facilitate learning (Bergmann, 2000; Karasek & Theorell, 1990; Mikkelsen, Saksvik, Eriksen, & Ursin, 1999). Karasek and Theorell (1990) argued that one of the most important determinants of productivity in mental work is related to job characteristics that offer the opportunity to learn and to develop one's skills. High efficiency occurs among incumbents of high demands/high control jobs. Working in these (active) jobs should be associated with active learning and feelings of mastery, which in turn buffers the development of strain and thus over time, leading to improved health. Health is seen as a necessary precondition for high job performance, since ill-health reduces the employee's ability to work efficiently. However, a restriction for the validity of this learning hypothesis, as formulated by Karasek and Theorell, is presented by Taris, Kompier, de Lange, Schaufeli, and Schreurs (2003). They showed that the highest levels of learning were not found for high demands/high control jobs, but rather for low demands/high control jobs.

In this study personal development was defined as the improvement of skills and knowledge. Thus, opportunities for personal development refer to whether a job provides opportunities for learning or not. Considering learning as one of the outcomes of work is in line with the view that humans change and develop while interacting with their (work) environment (Baltes, Staudinger, & Lindenberger, 1999; Leontjew, 1978). Thus, a job that facilitates learning does not mean that employees are sent on a training or course to acquire new knowledge, but rather that they learn while they are working (Bergmann, 2000). Opportunities to learn at work usually depend on the extent to which job incumbents have the freedom to make decisions about their time and about the procedures they would like to use to carry out their work (including individual goal setting). Other relevant aspects are whether the job incumbent has responsibility for the his/her own work process and the results of his/her actions, and whether he/she receives adequate feedback on his/her actions. Specific feedback is important as it allows the person to make a comparison between the goals he/she has set for him/herself and what (s)he has achieved so far (see action regulation theory by Hacker, 2002). Individuals are able to learn from the results of their own actions, when they are given decision authority and the opportunity to choose their own way of executing their work tasks (Mikkelsen et al., 1999). These learning opportunities can be measured with self-report methods based on items (e.g., "I have the opportunity to learn new skills in my work"). However, the usage of subjective methods is based upon two assumptions. The first assumption is that people know what the meaning of the item is that they are replying to and this meaning should be shared between people. The second assumption is that perceptions about the characteristics of the job (and thus about learning opportunities) are not affected by other factors. Usually peoples' perceptions are also influenced by what other people think (Salancik & Pfeffer, 1977), and also by their ability to reflect on the level of their skills and knowledge. Often the above-mentioned assumptions are not valid. Furthermore, when job incumbents are asked to rate their learning opportunities at work, it is not entirely clear which cognitive representations of the construct "learning opportunities" the person has, and thus it is not clear what one would actually measure. Therefore, asking people's assessments of job characteristics that constitute learning opportunities does not solve this problem, but only makes the problem of cognitive representations more complex.

Therefore, preference was given to an indirect and more objective assessment of learning opportunities. Learning opportunities were operationalized, based on Action Theoretical principles (Hacker, 1986, 1993), as objectively measurable job characteristics.

As stated at the beginning of this article, efficiency improvement is expected when work is designed in such a way that it facilitates learning and health. Thus, the question arises whether job characteristics that give the employees learning opportunities are also associated with better health. Before investigating this question, we should first define how health can be measured in the work context. A simple definition of health is the absence of illness, accidents, and strain (Ottawa Charter, 1986). Therefore, one way of measuring health is by looking at information as the number, type, and seriousness of reported diagnoses as well as the number and duration of hospitalizations and surgical operations during a predefined period (such measures are widely used by health insurance companies; Mossey & Roos, 1987).

A second way to assess health might be to analyse physiological processes and measuring physiological parameters. In ergonomics, cardiovascular parameters have been introduced to evaluate the consequences of having been exposed to workload and strain (e.g., Luczak, 1987; Schnall, Schwartz, Landsbergis, Warren, & Pickering, 1998; Theorell, Ahlberg-Hulten, Jodko, Sigala, & Torre, 1993; Theorell et al., 1991). In order to use cardiovascular parameters as an indicator for health, both the situation of exposure to workload and the process of recovery after exposure to workload should be taken into account. The process of recovery can be considered as an indicator of good health. An indication of good health is when a person can recover completely from workload within the timeframe between two working days (Rau, 2004; Ulich & Wülser, 2004). This definition is supported by the model of allostasis and allostatic load (McEwen, 1998; Sterling & Eyer, 1988). Allostasis describes the process of how the physiological system adjusts from one level of activation to the other, including the change from activity to rest (Sterling, 2004). The physiological system is continuously changing in order to adapt to the change in circumstances. Through this continuous change the system tries to achieve a level of stability. A healthy response of an allostatic system (such as the central and vegetative nervous system, the endocrine and immune system, the cardiovascular system, etc.) to exposure of load consists of three steps: (a) initiate a response to adapt to the current demanding situation, (b) sustaining this response reaction until the demanding situation comes to an end and the load ends, and (c) shutting off the response after the demand is no longer imposed on the system. The system will than come to a state of rest (McEwan, 1998). For example, an adaptive response to workload could be an increase in heart rate and blood pressure for the duration of the demanding situation. Once the demands are gone and the person no longer faces the workload, heart rate and blood pressure must be reset, i.e., enter a state of rest (Pickering, 1997).

However, allostatic load situations occur when the initial adaptive response fails to be shut off after the load has gone (e.g., blood pressure remains elevated up to the late night). Allostatic load is thus considered to be a pathophysiological outcome (McEwan, 1998; Sterling & Eyer, 1988).

Consequently, a distinction between a "healthy" and an "unhealthy" reaction to workload can be made based on how the organism responds to load and the reaction afterwards. Healthy (allostasis) and unhealthy (allostatic) responses to load can be distinguished for various physiological systems. In this study we looked at the allostasis of the cardiovascular system; in particular we looked at how heart rate and blood pressure responded to exposure to workload and how these parameters changed after work during the night.

However, health is more than absence of illness. Therefore, a third way of measuring health is to ask people about their general health and well-being (e.g., GHQ; Goldberg, 1992; Goldberg & Williams, 1988), mental health (e.g., TPF; Becker, 1989), life satisfaction (e.g., SWEL; Diener, Emmons, Larsen, & Griffin, 1985), and vocational success (Schaarschmidt & Fischer, 1997). For these variables it has been demonstrated that they are linked to a wide range of physical and mental complaints, as well as health behaviours. For example, studies showed that mental health was negatively related to low level of physical complaints (Becker, 2000) and anxiety (Becker, 1989).

Furthermore, both mental health (Becker, 1989) and life satisfaction (Herrman et al., 2002) were negatively correlated with depressive symptoms. In studies among entrepreneurs (Kieschke & Schaarschmidt, 2003) and teachers (Schaarschmidt & Fischer, 1998) vocational success was used as an indicator for good health. This confirms findings by Becker (2000), who reported that feelings of success results from good mental health.

Considering the limitations of each of the above-described methods to measure health (absence of illness or limitation, allostasis, and feelings of well-being), it seems recommendable to use more than one method.

In this study we will use the objective and subjective measure of allostasis and the subjective measure of well-being and mental health. A full cardiovascular recovery after load (i.e., a healthy response to load) is considered to be an objective indicator of allostasis. The self-reported ability to recover and the absence of sleeping problems will be considered as a subjective indicator for allostasis.

The aim of this study is to test whether job characteristics that facilitate learning are positively related to health outcomes. Based on the allostasis model (see above) we assume that a healthy person should be able to recover completely within the time frame between two working days (Rau, 2004; Ulich & Wülser, 2004). Recovery can be measured by objective and subjective indicators. An objective indicator is the change in cardiovascular activity (heart rate, blood pressure) after the workload has come to an end (Pickering, 1997; Sterling, 2004). Thus, it is hypothesized that:

H1:   The more learning opportunities are available in a job, the better will be the nocturnal recovery of cardiovascular activity after workload.

Subjective health outcomes in the framework of the allostasis model are the ability to relax, and the absence of sleeping problems.

H2:   The more learning opportunities are available in a job, the less sleep disturbances will be reported and the higher will be the ability to relax.

More unspecific subjective health-outcomes are self-rated mental health, life satisfaction, and vocational success.

H3:   The more learning opportunities are available in a job, the better will be the person's mental health and life satisfaction, as well as the higher the vocational success.

The relationship between the objectively assessed learning opportunities and health may be moderated by the job incumbents' perception of the opportunities to learn at work. Thus, it is necessary to control for subjective perceptions of learning opportunities. As a measure for subjectively perceived learning opportunities we used self-rated decision latitude (e.g., Karasek et al., 1998; Richter, Hemmann, Merboth, Fritz, & Hänsgen, 2000). Furthermore, the experience of time pressure and work intensity should be controlled for, since high time pressure and high level of work intensity prevent use being made of existing learning opportunities (Taris et al., 2003). Thus the fourth and fifth hypotheses are:

H4:   Perceived decision latitude will moderate the relationship between objectively measured learning opportunities and health. The more decision latitude job incumbents experience, the stronger will be the relation between objective learning opportunities and health.

H5:   Perceived time pressure and high work intensity (job demands) will moderate the relationship between objectively measured learning opportunities and health. The more time pressure and work intensity job incumbents are experiencing, the weaker will be the relationship between objective learning opportunities and health.

METHOD

Participants

Participants were 185 healthy workers, employed in white-collar jobs in the electronic chip industry, multimedia companies, insurance companies, and public service. Of these, 85 were female and 100 male. The average age of women was 38.8 ($SD = 10.3$), and that of men 36.7 ($SD = 8.9$). Participants had an employment contract stipulating a weekly working time of 38–40 hours.

Participants were recruited through presentations in the companies and by e-mails sent via companies' intranet. All participants were paid 25 euros for taking part in the study.

Assessment of learning opportunities at work

As job characteristics that support learning at work, the temporal and procedural autonomy of employees with respect to executing work tasks, decision authority, responsibility, feedback about one's own actions and about results were selected. These six job characteristics were assessed with the Task Diagnosis Survey (TDS; Pohlandt, Hacker, & Richter, 1999; Rudolph, Schönfelder, & Hacker, 1987). The TDS is an instrument for job analysis, based on Hacker's model of action regulation (Hacker, 1986,

2003). It is considered to be an "objective" method, because it is independent of the job incumbent's perception of his/her work task. An experienced job analyst has assessed the following six job characteristics for each of the 185 participants:

- *Procedural degrees of freedom*. This dimension refers to the degrees of freedom the job incumbent has in deciding what subtasks should be worked on, in which sequence they should be executed, and which tools to use; and to what extent the job incumbent can influence the outcomes of the work process. (This implies that the job incumbent knows how to do the task.)
- *Temporal degrees of freedom*. This dimension refers to degrees of freedom regarding the time used for executing subtasks and available amount of time between subtasks.
- *Decision authority*. This dimension refers to whether job incumbents can develop and select their own working methods for the task. A high level of procedural degrees of freedom (the first dimension) is a precondition for decision authority.
- *Responsibility*. This dimension describes what kind of responsibility the job incumbent has at work (e.g., no responsibility, responsibility for quantity and quality of outputs, responsibility for work of other people, responsibility for safety and health of other people).
- *Information about results*. This dimension refers to amount of information the employee can obtain during the work process about the anticipated results of his/her own work process. And also information about the work processes of colleagues can be relevant when these work processes are related (interdependency). Such information enhances the transparency of the work process and thus the task.
- *Feedback*. This dimension refers to the effectiveness of feedback. Effective feedback is extensive and specific. The feedback should specify the progress of the work process and the results of the activities. Whereas the previous dimension focuses on information that is related to understand the position of the individual's task from the perspective of the whole technological process, this dimension provides specific information about the job incumbent's own work process and his/her progress (e.g., failures, quality, etc.).

Expert analysts rated the jobs on these dimensions, using equivalent scales. The six scales differ in their number of scale points. Each scale point has an anchor with a specific description of the implementation of that task requirement (see an example in the Appendix). The basis of the job analyst's rating was information collected by reading documents about the job and by interviewing and observing the job incumbent. In addition, the job incumbent's supervisor has been interviewed. Specifically, documents used by the job analyst were job descriptions, work contracts, and documents about the structure of the organization. Learning opportunities were operationalized by calculating a sum score over the z-normalized values of the TDS-scales.

The interrater reliability and test–retest reliability for different jobs were reported for each scale of the Task Diagnosis Survey (Hacker, Fritsche, Richter, & Iwanowa, 1995). Interrater reliability coefficients for the six scales defining learning opportunities were between $r = .64$ and 1.0. The test–retest reliability coefficients for these scales were between $r = .88$ and 1.0.

Self reports about job characteristics (perceived decision latitude and job demands)

Each participant assessed the amount of decision latitude and job demands for his/her job by means of the FIT-questionnaire (questionnaire and results concerning its development and validity were published in Richter et al., 2000). The first draft of this questionnaire was developed in 1980 based on the items reported by Karasek (1979). Therefore there is semantic agreement between the German FIT items for job demand and decision latitude and the corresponding JCQ items. However, the correlation between both questionnaires has not been examined so far.

The FIT-questionnaire operationalizes decision latitude and job demands as follows:

- *Decision latitude.* Seven items about procedural and temporal degrees of freedom, and skill utilization (Cronbach's alpha $= .81$; retest reliability, $r = .69$, Richter et al., 2000).
- *Job demands.* Six items about work intensity, extensive work, time pressure, and difficulty of work (Cronbach's alpha $= .73$; retest reliability $r = .67$, Richter et al., 2000).

All items were scored on a Likert scale from 1 ("not at all") to 4 ("completely"). Decision latitude and job demand are each defined as the quotient of their summed items and the number of items.

Assessment of health

In this study both objective and subjective health parameters were assessed. Since our health definition was based on the allostasis model (see introduction), recovery after load had to be assessed.

Objective health indicators. Two cardiovascular parameters were used as indicators for health: blood pressure and heart rate. According the allostasis model these parameters should be measured during load at day time and during recovery at night time. Therefore, blood pressure and heart rate were recorded over a 24-hour period by ambulatory monitoring. Additionally, motor activity was recorded to control for confounding effects on cardiovascular activity. More specifically, blood pressure readings were automatically recorded every 15 minutes throughout the day and every 30 minutes during the first 2 hours of night sleep, and every 60 minutes during the rest of the night (blood pressure monitor BOSO TM2420; readings taken by the Korotkoff method). Heart rate was recorded continuously together with motor activity by using a two-channel ambulatory monitor (Physiomodul by MedNatic). Additional information concerning motor activity was obtained via a little diary. Participants were issued with a handheld computer, containing the diary. With specific intervals questions as "where are you", "what do you do", etc., were prompted, to which the participant had to respond. The assessment of recovery is based on the reduction of nocturnal systolic and diastolic blood pressure, and the reduction of heart rate during the night. The nocturnal reduction rates (NRR) represent the nocturnal change in blood pressure and heart rate in relation to the mean level during the day time. NRR is calculated according to the following formula (Li et al., 1997):

$$\text{NRR } (\%) = [(\text{day time mean} - \text{night time mean})/\text{day time mean}] \times 100$$

When the level of blood pressure is not reduced during the night, this is an indication of allostatic load, which can lead to accelerated atherosclerosis. Therefore, participants were divided into two groups according to whether both systolic and diastolic blood pressure dropped during the night. All participants whose blood pressure dropped more than 10% during night time compared to their day time level were diagnosed as "dipper" (NRR > 10%; healthy response, e.g., allostasis). And all participants whose blood pressure dropped less than 10% compared to day time level (NRR ≤ 10%; not healthy response, e.g., allostatic load) were diagnosed as "nondippers". Whereas thresholds have been published for "healthy" (dipper) versus "not-healthy" (nondipper) drops in nocturnal blood pressure, there are no thresholds published to classify "healthy" versus "not healthy" drops in nocturnal heart rate.

Subjective health indicators. Participants' assessment of their ability to relax, and their assessment of sleep quality (i.e., how undisturbed their sleep has been) were used as subjective health indicators. Ability to relax was assessed using the FABA-questionnaire (Richter, Rudolph, & Schmidt, 1996). The "ability to relax" scale of the FABA-questionnaire

(Cronbach's alpha = .79; test – retest reliability ranges from $r = .62$ to $r = .74$) consists of six Likert-scale items, with four response categories ranging from "strongly agree" to "strongly disagree" (e.g., "I find it difficult to 'switch off' after work", "I often have trouble falling asleep because problems of my work keep going through my mind"). Norm values for normal and for disturbed ability to relax have been developed for this instrument (Richter et al., 1996). These norm values are dependent on age and gender. Thus, age and gender need to be taken into account when a distinction is made between participants who were able to relax, and those whose ability to relax was disturbed.

Sleep complaints were assessed with the Sleep Wake Experience List (SWEL; van Diest, 1990), which asks about sleep related complaints during the last 3 months. Reliabilities of the SWEL are average to high, with kappa ranging from 52.3% to 90.3% for various sleep complaints in a clinical validation study (van Diest, 1990). Both the incidence and severity of the complaints were assessed with 18 items. Examples of sleep complaints that are tested with SWEL are problems with falling asleep, problems with maintaining sleep, waking up early in the morning, etc. The SWEL defined norm values for each sleep problem, and for the general diagnosis of disturbed sleep. In this study all kinds of sleep disturbances classified by SWEL were summarized into one category, i.e., "sleep disturbances". Participants with and without sleep disturbances were compared.

In addition to their own assessment of their recovery, participants were also asked to rate various aspects of their general health, such as mental health, life satisfaction, and vocational success. Mental health was defined by the ability to cope with external and internal psychological demands. This was measured with the Mental Health scale of the Trier Personality Questionnaire (TPF; Becker, 1989). The TPF consist of 20 items that are scored on 4-point Likert scales, with response categories ranging from "not at all" to "always" (Cronbach's alpha = .91; retest reliability $r = .77$). Life satisfaction and vocational success were measured with the AVEM-questionnaire (Schaarschmidt & Fischer, 1997). The life satisfaction scale (Cronbach's alpha = .84; retest reliability $r = .81$) and the vocational success scale (Cronbach's alpha = .82; retest reliability $r = .73$.) consist each of six items, scored on 5-point Likert scales, each ranging from "not at all" to "completely".

Procedure

Three data-recorded sessions were organized with each participant. In the following the typical procedure is described. On the first day the participant's job was analysed by an expert at the workplace). Then, participants were asked to complete questionnaires regarding sociodemographic data, their job characteristics, ability to relax, sleep disturbances, and general aspects of health.

On the second day, the 24-hour period of ambulatory monitoring started. This day, participants arrived in the laboratory (which was set up in the companies) between 7 and 8 a.m. The ambulatory equipment was put on and the participant was instructed with respect to blood pressure readings (keep the arm as motionless as possible) and how to use the handheld computer to complete the diary. Participants then started their regular working day for 8 hours, with subsequent free time in the afternoon and the evening, and sleep at night.

After the 24 hours of ambulatory assessment (on the third day), participant returned to the laboratory. The physiological data and the data of the handheld computer were transferred to the laboratory computer.

Whereas the job analysis and completing the questionnaires (first day) could take place on any regular working day before the 24-hour ambulatory assessment, the ambulatory assessment itself had to take place on two successive working days (second and third day).

Preparation of physiological data for statistical analysis

Time at work was derived from the diary information of the handheld computers and the protocols after exploring the 24-hour ambulatory monitoring data. Night-time was defined as the time between going to bed and getting up as participants had indicated with the diary. This information was verified by the data on motor activity from the ambulatory monitoring. Artifacts were excluded (artifacts for systolic blood pressure—SBP, diastolic blood pressure—DBP, and heart rate—bpm, were defined as any of the following: $SBP < 50$ mmHg, $SBP > 250$ mmHg, $DBP > SBP$, $DBP < 30$ mmHg, $DBP > 150$ mmHg, $HR < 40$ bpm, and those segments that were confounded by high level of motor activity). The readings for systolic and diastolic blood pressure and for heart rate within day-time and night-time were separately averaged.

Statistical analyses

In order to test the first two hypotheses, which stated that jobs with learning opportunities provide better opportunities for recovery according the allostasis model (Hypotheses 1 and 2) hierarchical linear regression analysis were performed to assess the contribution of job characteristics in predicting reduction of nocturnal heart rate. Hierarchical logistic regression analyses were used to assess the contribution of job characteristics to predict dipping status, ability to relax, and sleep disturbances. Hierarchical linear regression analyses were performed to assess the contribution of job characteristics to predict aspects of health: mental health, life satisfaction, and vocational success (Hypothesis 3). For the independent variables a distinction was made between "objective" data (learning opportunities at work, age, gender, body mass index[1]) and the self-rated (subjective) work variables. All regression analyses were based on three blocks:

- Block 1 included the objectively determined data: learning opportunities, gender, age, and body mass index (bmi).
- Block 2 included the self-rated work variables: decision latitude, job demands.
- Block 3 included the two-way interactions between learning opportunities and decision latitude, and between learning opportunities and job demands.

Block 3 was entered to examine whether perceived decision latitude (Hypothesis 4) or perceived time pressure (Hypothesis 5) moderate the relationship between learning opportunities and health.

RESULTS

Table 1 shows means, standard deviations, and zero-order correlations between the expert ratings and self-report assessments of work characteristics. Expert ratings of learning opportunities are highly correlated with self-reports of decision latitude, but much lower with job demands. However, decision latitude and job demands are not independent of each other. The higher the job demands, the higher the decision latitude.

Objective health (recovery Hypothesis 1)

Results of the linear regression analysis to predict nocturnal reduction rate of heart rate are presented in Table 2. From the personal variables entered in Block 1, the variables age ($R^2 = .096$), body mass index ($R^2 = .030$), and learning opportunities ($R^2 = .103$) remained in the model. The two self-rated job variables, job demands and decision latitude (Block 2), were not significantly associated with the nocturnal reduction of heart rate. Nor was the interaction between learning opportunities and decision latitude (Block 3).

---

[1]Since body weight (in relation to body size) has a strong effect on cardiovascular parameters (e.g., Kannel, Brand, Skinner, Dawber, & McNamara, 1967; Sowers, 1998), body mass index (bmi) was used as an additional control variable in statistical analyses of cardiovascular variables. Bmi was calculated as: weight/height^2 (with weight in kilograms; height in metres).

TABLE 1

Means, standard deviations, and zero-order correlations between the objectively and subjectively rated work characteristics

| | | | Work characteristics | |
| | | | Learning opportunities | Decision latitude |
Work characteristics	M	SD		
Objective				
Learning opportunities	0.23	3.74	—	
Self-report				
Decision latitude	3.07	0.49	.539****	—
Job demands	2.50	0.55	.208**	.321****

$N = 183$; **$p < .01$; ****$p < .001$.
Skill utilization and decision authority are subscales of decision latitude.

TABLE 2

Results of the regression analyses predicting nocturnal heart rate reduction (method forward)

Prediction of: Block	Step	Variable	R^2	ΔR^2	B	B'	p
NRR of HF							
Block 1	Step 1	Age	.096	.096	−.200	−.263	.000
	Step 2	Learning opportunities	.199	.103	.642	.329	.000
	Step 3	Body mass index	.230	.030	−.419	−.184	.014
Blocks 2–3		No variable was significantly associated					

$N = 162$; B = standardized beta coefficient at the current step; B' = standardized beta coefficient at the step where the last variable was entered in the model.

Binary logistic regression (method: forward *Wald*) was used to identify variables that are associated with the risk of being a "nondipper" versus "dipper" with respect to blood pressure status ("dipper": participants with nocturnal reduction rate of blood pressure $> 10\%$; "nondipper": participants with nocturnal reduction rate $\leq 10\%$).

From all personal variables entered in Block 1, only the variable learning opportunities remained in the logistic regression model (Table 3). More specifically, the "initial log likelihood"-value was 195.05. After entering the learning opportunities in the first step, the "-2-Log Likelihood" value decreased to 189.41 (Cox & Snell $R^2 = .05$). The chi-squared of the model was significant (chi-squared = 5.64, $p = .018$). The odds ratio, Exp(B), is 1.12. This means that when the independent variable "learning opportunities" decreases one unit, the odds that the dependent is "nondipper"

TABLE 3
Wald statistic to test the significance for each of the independent variables in the logistic
regression model for prediction of dipping status

Block	Variables	B	SD	Wald	df	p	Exp(B)	95% CI Lower	95% CI Upper
Block 1	Step 1 Learning opportunities	.11	.05	5.54	1	.019	1.12	1.02	1.22
Blocks 2−3	No variable was significantly associated								

$N = 181$.
   Dependent variable is the dipping-status (dipper = 1; nondipper = 0). The independent
variables are personal variables (Block 1: learning opportunities, gender, body mass index,
gender), self-reports about work (Block 2: job demands, decision latitude), interaction of
learning opportunities with decision latitude (Block 3).

increases by a factor of 1.12. In other words, the participant whose job had
the lowest learning opportunities had a 7.93 times higher risk of being a
nondipper than the participant who worked in the job with the highest
learning opportunities (the range of the variable "learning opportunities" is
from -9.51 to 8.76 and $1.12^{18.3} = 7.93$). Neither self-rated job characteristics nor the interaction between learning opportunities and self-rated
decision latitude were significantly associated with dipper status.

Subjective health (self-rated recovery variables Hypothesis 2)

The binary regression analysis with sleep disturbances as dependent variable
yielded no significant results for any of the tested variables (*Wald* statistic,
method forward; all independent variables were dropped from the model).
   Results of the binary logistic regression analyses for the prediction of the
ability to relax are shown in Table 4. Only job demands (Block 2) significantly predicted the ability to relax. In detail, the "-2-Log Likelihood" value
decreased from the "initial log likelihood"-value of 174.88 to 164.71 (Cox &
Snell $R^2 = .088$). The chi-squared of the model was highly significant
(chi-squared = 10.17, $p = .002$). This means that when the job demands
increases by one unit, the risk of a disturbed ability to relax increases by a
factor of 3.25 (see Table 4). Since job demands are scored from 1.00 to 4.00,
the risk of having a disturbed ability to relax is 34.33 times higher for the
participant with the highest job demands than for the participant with the
lowest job demands (the difference between lowest and highest job demands
is three units, and $3.25^3 = 34.33$). Neither learning opportunities nor
demographic variables (Block 1) were entered into the model. There was

TABLE 4
Wald statistic to test the significance for each of the independent variables in the logistic
regression model for prediction of a disturbed ability to relax

								95% CI	
Block	Variables	B	SD	Wald	df	p	Exp(B)	Lower	Upper
Block 1		No variable was significantly associated							
Block 2	Step 1 Job demands[a]	1.18	0.39	9.17	1	.002	3.25	1.52	6.96
Block 3						Ns			

$N = 181$.

Dependent variable is the disturbed ability to relax, which is coded 1 = disturbed ability to relax, 0 = ability to relax.

[a]Job demands score ranges from 1.00 to 4.00.

also no interaction effect between learning opportunities and self-rated decision latitude on the ability to relax (Block 3).

Subjective health (general health variables Hypothesis 3)

Table 5 shows the results of the linear regression analyses to predict the various aspects of general health: "mental health", "life satisfaction", and "vocational success".

Mental health was exclusively predicted by decision latitude ($B = .32$, $p < .000$). No other variable entered the regression model.

Gender (B at current step $= -.23$, $p < .01$) and decision latitude ($B = B' = .36$, $p < .000$) significantly predicted *life satisfaction* (with men being more life satisfied). However, gender became nonsignificant when decision latitude was entered (B' at highest step $= -.08$, $p = .318$). Learning opportunities or the interaction of learning opportunities with decision latitude was not significantly associated with life satisfaction.

Learning opportunities (B at current step $= .38$, $p = .000$) and decision latitude (B at current step $= .47$, $p = .000$) explained, with 15% and 16% respectively, a significant proportion of variance in *vocational success*.

DISCUSSION

The aim of this study was to test whether objectively assessed job characteristics, which are known as prerequisites for learning (defined here as "learning opportunities") contribute to health outcomes.

Learning opportunities at work were assessed as objectively as possible, with the help of experts, who assessed those job characteristics that are

TABLE 5
Results of the regression analyses for predicting self-rated health characteristics
(method forward)

Prediction of: Block	Step	Variable	R^2	ΔR^2	B	B'
Mental health						
Block 1			No variable was significantly associated			
Block 2	Step 1	Decision latitude	.10	.10	.32***	.60***
Block 3				ns		
Life satisfaction						
Block 1	Step 1	Gender	.05	.05	− .23**	− .08
Block 2	Step 2	Decision latitude	.16	.11		.36***
Block 3				ns		
Vocational success						
Block 1	Learning opportunities		.15	.15	.38***	.13*
Block 2	Decision latitude		.31	.16	.47***	
Block 3				ns		

Only significant variables are presented. *$p < .05$; **$p < .01$; ***$p < .001$.
$N = 179$; $B =$ standardized beta coefficient at the current step; $B' =$ standardized beta coefficient at the step where the last variable was entered in the model.

known from the literature as prerequisites for learning. Health was operationalized, according the allostasis model (McEwan, 1998), as the ability of the body to adjust to the change between the states of resting and being active (allostasis). For example, the different physiological systems should change their activation from workload to nocturnal rest. A healthy response is reflected by a decrease in blood pressure when the workload has ended and a situation of rest starts (allostasis). An unhealthy response (i.e., allostatic load) can be noted when the blood pressure fails to decrease when the load situation ends and rest starts (Sterling, 2004). This leads to a situation of sustained activation, which is closely associated with becoming ill (hypertension, stroke, etc.) (McEwan, 1998).

In this study the change of cardiovascular activation from workload to nocturnal rest was used as an objective indicator for recovery after work. Subjective indicators for recovery were self-reports on the ability to relax and the absence of sleep disturbances. As subjective indicators for general health participants' assessments of their mental health, life satisfaction, and vocational success were used.

The main finding in the present study was that health is associated with the objectively assessed learning opportunities at work. However, there were differences in the relationship. In support of Hypothesis 1, learning opportunities were associated with nocturnal recovery of heart rate and blood pressure. However, in contrast to Hypothesis 2 learning opportunities were not associated with self-rated assessments of recovery, i.e., ability to relax and sleep disturbances. In detail, results for Hypothesis 1 show that more learning opportunities at work result in a stronger proportional reduction of heart rate during the night. The variance explained by learning opportunities (10%) was higher than that of the biological variables age (9.6%) and body mass index (3%). A similar result was found for the prediction of dippers (participants with healthy blood pressure recovery) and nondippers (those with nonhealthy recovery). Thus, the employees' dipping status was exclusively predicted by learning opportunities. Participants with high learning opportunities had a significantly lower risk of being nondippers than those with low learning opportunities. The mechanism by which learning opportunities contribute to increased nocturnal recovery is not clear. However, at least two possible mechanisms should be discussed. Firstly, jobs with learning opportunities can be considered as intrinsically motivating and positively challenging for the job incumbents (Czicksentmihalyi, 1990; Hacker, 2003; Karasek & Theorell, 1990). People in such jobs usually are highly activated, but not stressed. At the end of their working day they should be able to adjust to the situation of rest (i.e., unwind) and recover completely during the night. An explanation might be that since these people have control over their work, they can decide themselves how to deal with problems, and when to stop working. Apparently this helps them better to switch off from work (see Cropley, Dijk, & Stanley, 2006 this issue; Sonnentag & Kruel, 2006 this issue), which helps them to unwind. Unwinding is accompanied by a reduction of nocturnal heart rate and blood pressure. On the other hand, people in jobs without learning opportunities have reduced degrees of freedom and hardly any decision authority. More generally, people in such jobs have less control over their work. That means that the strain potential of those jobs is high. It is well known that high job strain is associated with elevated blood pressure and heart rate as compared to situations with low job strain (Cesana et al., 2003; Gerin, Litt, Deich, & Pickering, 1995) and also with delayed recovery (Dienstbier, 1989; Haynes, Gannon, Orimoto, O'Brien, & Brandt, 1991; Rau, Georgiades, Lemne, de Faire, & Fredrikson, 2001).

In contrast to the positive relationship between learning opportunities and objective health parameters, no relationship was found between subjective health parameters and learning opportunities (rejection of Hypothesis 2). Neither ability to relax nor sleep disturbances were related to learning opportunities. Thus, learning opportunities in the job affect physiological recovery but not the subjective experience of recovery. An explanation for this finding can only be speculative. Since the ability to relax was exclusively affected by self-rated job demands, it might well be that when people perceive the job demands as high (thus causing strain), this might prevent them from learning anything (accepting Hypothesis 5). This is actually predicted by the extended Job–Control model (Karasek & Theorell, 1990). So, the effect of job demands on the ability to relax could have masked the effects of learning opportunities since the effect of job demands was stronger.

The results showed that with high job demands the risk of not being able to relax increases. This result is also in line with findings by Cropley and Purvis (2003) who found a positive relationship between job demands and rumination, Appels (1997) who demonstrated that high job demands are related to inability to relax and exhaustion, and Sonnentag (2001) who reported that high level of job demands are related to decreased situational well-being before going to sleep. However, it has to be taken into account that the constructs of rumination and situational well-being before going to bed are related to the construct ability to relax, but they are not similar.

Less support was found for Hypothesis 3. General health aspects were not affected by learning opportunities. Only vocational success appeared to be significantly related to learning opportunities. The more learning opportunities the job had, the higher the rating of vocational success. A logical explanation is that the use of the knowledge that has been acquired while executing the job increases the efficiency and effectiveness of the incumbent. Both the higher level of efficiency at work and the feeling of increased competence can lead to the experience of vocational success.

The other two health variables, mental health and life satisfaction, were not related to the expert's assessments of learning opportunities but to the self-rated job characteristics. Self-rated decision latitude appeared to be the best predictor for all self-rated health related variables. The linear regression analyses revealed that decision latitude was a significant predictor for each of the dependent variables, accounting for 11% of the variance in life satisfaction, 10% in mental health, and 16% in vocational success. These findings support earlier studies on the relationship between (self-rated) decision latitude with self-reports on mental health (de Croon, van der Beek, Blonk, & Frings-Dresen, 2000; Warr, 1990), job satisfaction (Petterson, Arnetz, & Arnetz, 1995), and life satisfaction (Kalimo & Vuori, 1990).

Since hardly any studies used objective assessments of job characteristics and objective parameters of health, there are no studies to compare our results with, and thus the discussion has a speculative element. It is acknowledged that the use of self-reports as indicators of the objective environment is often inaccurate (Spector, 1992). The same applies to self-reports of health (Myrtek, 1998). However, intercorrelations between self-reported data are generally higher then correlations between objective and subjective measures (Spector, 1992). This could be a reason for the finding that self-reported health is related to self-reported decision latitude but not to objectively measured learning opportunities.

It was hypothesized (Hypothesis 4) that decision latitude is a moderator of the relationship between learning opportunities and health. This hypothesis had to be rejected for the relationship between learning opportunities and all the health parameters regarding recovery. Although participants working in jobs with higher learning opportunities perceived higher decision latitude, the interaction between learning opportunities and decision latitude did not explain additional variance in the prediction of health variables. It seems that objectively assessed job characteristics are more important for health than what people think of their job.

Study limitations

There is no generally accepted operationalization of learning opportunities. In this study an expert assessment of learning opportunities in the job was used. Action Theory was used to operationalize learning opportunities and to help experts to assess those job characteristics that facilitate learning at work. However, we do not know whether people who objectively had the opportunity to learn actually also did learn. Measuring learning effects is difficult since criteria for learning must be defined. When questionnaires are used to measure whether people have learned something, it requires that people think or know that they indeed have learned something. However, perceptions of learning can be affected by many other factors.

Objective health parameters were only measured with regard to the cardiovascular system. However, parameters of other physiological systems, like the endocrinological or the immunological system, can shed further light on the relationship between job aspects that are conducive to learning and health.

CONCLUSION

Work psychology has as a general goal to design jobs that (1) facilitate personal development and (2) are conducive to health. The current study supports the notion that both aspects, personal development and health, are related. Moreover, it can be concluded that in order to evaluate whether these goals have been achieved, it is recommendable to use both objective assessments of work design and objective parameters of health. However, before designing or redesigning jobs with regard to these aims, the construct of "personal development" has to be specified. First the question should be answered: Which specific aspects of the person should be developed?

REFERENCES

Appels, A. (1997). Exhausted subjects, exhausted systems. *Acta Physiologica Scandinavica, Supplementum, 640*, 153 – 154.

Baltes, P. B., Staudinger, U. M., & Lindenberger, U. (1999). Life-span developmental psychology. *Annual Review of Psychology, 50*, 471 – 507.

Becker, P. (1989). *Trierer Persönlichkeitsfragebogen (TPF)*. Göttingen, Germany: Hogrefe.

Becker, P. (2000). Die "Big Two" Seelische Gesundheit und Verhaltenskontrolle: zwei orthogonale Superfaktoren höherer Ordnung? *Zeitschrift für Differentielle und Diagnostische Psychologie, 21*, 113 – 124.

Bergmann, B. (2000). Kompetenzentwicklung im Arbeitsprozess [Competence development at work]. *Zeitschrift für Arbeitswissenschaften, 2*, 138 – 144.

Cesana, G., Sega, R., Ferrario, M., Chiodini, P., Corrao, G., & Mancia, G. (2003). Job strain and blood pressure in employed men and women: A pooled analysis of four northern Italian population samples. *Psychosomatic Medicine, 65*, 558 – 563.

Cropley, M., Dijk, D.-J., & Stanley, N. (2006). Job strain, work rumination, and sleep in school teachers. *European Journal of Work and Organizational Psychology, 15*(2), 181 – 196.

Cropley, M., & Purvis, L. J. M. (2003). Job strain and rumination about work issues during leisure time: A diary study. *European Journal of Work and Organizational Psychology, 12*, 195 – 208.

Csikszentmihalyi, M. (1990). *Flow: The psychology of optimal experience*. New York: Harper & Row.

De Croon, E. M., van der Beek, A. J., Blonk, R. W. B., & Frings-Dresen, M. H. W. (2000). Job stress and psychosomatic health complaints among Dutch truck drivers: A re-evaluation of Karasek's interactive job demand – control model. *Stress Medicine, 16*, 101 – 107.

Diener, E., Emmons, R., Larsen, R., & Griffin, S. (1985). The Satisfaction with Life Scale. *Journal of Personal Assessment, 49*, 71 – 75.

Dienstbier, R. A. (1989). Arousal and physiological toughness: Implications for mental and physical health. *Psychological Review, 1*, 84 – 100.

Gerin, W., Litt, M. D., Deich, J., & Pickering, T. G. (1995). Self-efficacy as a moderator of perceived control effects on cardiovascular reactivity: Is enhanced control always beneficial? *Psychosomatic Medicine, 57*, 390 – 397.

Goldberg, D. (1992). *General Health Questionnaire (GHQ-12)*. Windsor, UK: NFER-Nelson.

Golderberg, D., & Williams, P. (1988). *A user's guide to the General Health Questionnaire*. Windsor, UK: NFER-Nelson.

Hacker, W. (1986). *Arbeitspsychologie*. Bern, Switzerland: Huber.

Hacker, W. (1993). Objective work environment: Analysis and evaluation of objective work characteristics. In L. Levi & J. L. Petterson (Eds.), *A healthier work environment: Basic concepts and methods of measurement*. (pp. 42 – 57). Copenhagen, Denmark: WHO Regional Office for Europe.

Hacker, W. (2002). Action theory, psychological. In N. J. Smelser & P. B. Baltes (Eds.), *International encyclopedia of the social and behavioral sciences* (pp. 58 – 62). London: Elsevier.

Hacker, W. (2003). Action regulation theory: A practical tool for the design of modern work processes. *European Journal of Work and Organizational Psychology, 12*, 105 – 130.

Hacker, W., Fritsche, B., Richter, P., & Iwanowa, A. (1995). *Tätigkeitsbewertungssystem (TBS): Verfahren zur Bewertung und Gestaltung von Arbeitstätigkeiten [Task diagnosis survey: A method of job analysis, job evaluation and job design]*. Zürich, Switzerland: vdf.

Haynes, S. H., Gannon, L. R., Orimoto, L., O'Brien, H., & Brandt, M. (1991). Psychophysiological assessment of poststress recovery. *Journal of Consulting and Clinical Psychology, 3*, 356 – 365.

Herrman, H., Patrick, D. L., Diehr, P., Martin, M. L., Fleck, M., Simon, G. E., & Buesching, D. P. (2002). Longitudinal investigation of depression outcomes in primary care in six countries: The LIDO study. Functional status, health service use and treatment of people with depressive symptoms. *Psychological Medicine, 32,* 889–902.

Kalimo, R., & Vuori, J. (1990). Work and sense of coherence: Resources for competence and life satisfaction. *Behavioral Medicine, 16,* 76–89.

Kannel, W. B., Brand, M., Skinner, J. J. Jr., Dawber, T. R., & McNamara, P. M. (1967). The relation of adiposity to blood pressure and development of hypertension: The Framingham Study. *Annals of Internal Medicine, 67,* 48–59.

Karasek, R. (1979). Job demands, job decision latitude, and mental strain: Implications for job redesign. *Administrative Science Quarterly, 24,* 285–307.

Karasek, R., Brisson, C., Kawakami, N., Houtman, I., Bongers, P., & Amick, B. (1998). The Job Content Questionnaire (JCQ): An instrument for internationally comparative assessments of psychosocial job characteristics. *Journal of Occupational Health Psychology, 3,* 322–355.

Karasek, R., & Theorell, T. (1990). *Healthy work: Stress, productivity, and the reconstruction of working life.* New York: Basic Books.

Kieschke, U., & Schaarschmidt, U. (2003). Bewältigungsverhalten als eignungs-relevantes Merkmal bei Existenzgründern: Ergebnisse einer Längsschnittstudie. *Zeitschrift für Personalpsychologie, 2,* 107–117.

Leontjew, A. N. (1978). *Activity, consciousness, and personality.* Englewood Cliffs, NJ: Prentice Hall.

Li, B., Ijiri, H., Yin, D., Takusagawa, M., Iwasaki, H., Mochizuki, Y., et al. (1997). Circadian variation of blood pressure and heart rate in normotensive pre- and postmenopausal women. *Nippon Ronen Igakkai Zasshi, 34,* 793–797.

Luczak, H. (1987). Psychophysiologische Methoden zur Erfassung psychophysischer Beanspruchungszustaende [Psychophysiological methods for the assessment of psychophysical strain]. In U. Kleinbeck & J. Rutenfranz (Eds.), *Enzyklopaedie der Psychologie, Themenbereich D, Praxisgebiete, Serie III, Wirtschafts-, Organisations- und Arbeitspsychologie, Band 1* (pp. 185–259). Göttingen, Germany: Hogrefe.

McEwen, B. S. (1998). Stress, adaptation, and disease: Allostasis and allostatic load. *Annals of the New York Academy of Sciences, 840,* 33–44.

Mikkelsen, A., Saksvik, P. O., Eriksen, H. R., & Ursin, H. (1999). The impact of learning opportunities and decision authority on occupational health. *Work and Stress, 13,* 20–31.

Mossey, J. M., & Roos, L. L. (1987). Using insurance claims to measure health status: The Illness Scale. *Journal of Chronic Diseases, 40*(Suppl. 1), 41S–54S.

Myrtek, M. (1998). *Gesunde Kranke—kranke Gesunde. Psychophysiologie des Krankheitsverhaltens [Healthy sick people—sick healthy people: Psychophysiology of sick behaviour].* Bern, Switzerland: Huber.

Ottawa Charter. (1986, November). *Ottawa Charter for Health Promotion.* Paper presented at the first international conference on Health Promotion, Ottawa, Canada.

Petterson, I.-L., Arnetz, B. B., & Arnetz, J. E. (1995). Predictors of job satisfaction and job influence: Results from a national sample of Swedish nurses. *Psychotherapy and Psychosomatics, 64,* 9–19.

Pickering, T. (1997). Cardiovascular measures of allostatic load. In J. D. MacArthur & C. T. MacArthur (Eds.), *Research network on socioeconomic status and health.* Retrieved January 21, 2006 from http://www.macses.ucsf.edu/Research/Allostatic/notebook/allostatic.html

Pohlandt, A., Hacker, W., & Richter, P. (1999). Tätigkeitsbewertungssystem (TBS). In H. Dunckel (Ed.), *Handbuch psychologischer Arbeitsanalyseverfahren* (pp. 515–538). Zürich, Switzerland: vdf Hochschulverlag an der ETH.

Rau, R. (2004). Job strain or healthy work: A question of task design. *Journal of Occupational Health Psychology, 9,* 322–338.

Rau, R., Georgiades, A., Lemne, C., de Faire, U., & Fredrikson, M. (2001). Psychosocial work characteristics and perceived control in relation to cardiovascular rewind at night. *Journal of Occupational Health Psychology*, 6, 171–181.

Richter, P. (2000). Action regulation theory and socio-technical analysis: A design-oriented integration of efficiently and healthy work systems. *International Journal of Psychology*, 35, 207.

Richter, P., Hemmann, E., Merboth, H., Fritz, S., & Hänsgen, C. (2000). Das Erleben von Arbeitsintensität und Tätigkeitsspielraum—Entwicklung und Validierung eines Fragebogens zur orientierenden Analyse (FIT). *Zeitschrift für Arbeits- und Organisationspsychologie*, 44, 129–139.

Richter, P., Rudolph, M., & Schmidt, C. F. (1996). *Fragebogen zur Diagnostik belastungsrelevanter Anforderungsbewältigung (FABA)*. Frankfurt, Germany: SWETS.

Rudolph, E., Schönfelder, E., & Hacker, W. (1987). *Tätigkeitsbewertungssystem für geistige Arbeit mit/ohne Rechnerunterstützung (TBS-GA)*. Berlin, Germany: Psychodiagnostisches Zentrum an der Humboldt Universität/Göttingen: Hogrefe.

Salancik, K. G., & Pfeffer, J. (1977). An examination of need-satisfaction models of job attitudes. *Administrative Science Quarterly*, 23, 223–253.

Schaarschmidt, U., & Fischer, A. W. (1997). AVEM—ein diagnostisches Instrument zur Differenzierung von Typen gesundheitsrelevanten Verhaltens und Erlebens gegenüber der Arbeit [AVEM—a diagnostic measure for the differentiation of types of health-relevant work-related behaviour and experience]. *Zeitschrift für Differentielle und Diagnostische Psychologie*, 18, 3, 151–163.

Schaarschmidt, U., & Fischer, A. (1998). Diagnostik interindividueller Unterschiede in der psychischen Gesundheit von Lehrerinnen und Lehrern zum Zwecke einer differentiellen Gesundheitsförderung. In E. Bamberg, A. Ducki, & A.-M. Metz (Eds.), *Handbuch Betriebliche Gesundheitsförderung*. Göttingen, Germany: Verlag für Angewandte Psychologie.

Schnall, P. L., Schwartz, J. E., Landsbergis, P. A., Warren, K., & Pickering, T. G. (1998). A longitudinal study of job strain and ambulatory blood pressure: Results from a three-year follow-up. *Psychosomatic Medicine*, 60, 697–706.

Sonnentag, S. (2001). Work, recovery activities, and individual well-being: A diary study. *Journal of Occupational Health Psychology*, 6, 196–210.

Sonnentag, S., & Kruel, U. (2006). Psychological detachment from work during off-job time: The role of job stressors, job involvement, and recovery-related self-efficacy. *European Journal of Work and Organizational Psychology*, 15(2), 197–217.

Sowers, J. R. (1998). Obesity and cardiovascular disease. *Clinical Chemistry*, 44, 1821–1825.

Spector, P. E. (1992). A consideration of the validity of and meaning of self-report measures of job conditions. *International Review of Industrial and Organizational Psychology*, 7, 123–151.

Sterling, P. (2004). Principles of allostasis: Optimal design, predictive regulation, pathophysiology and rational therapeutics. In J. Schulkin (Ed.), *Allostasis, homeostasis, and the costs of adaptation* (pp. 2–36). Cambridge, UK: Cambridge University Press.

Sterling, P., & Eyer, J. (1988). Allostasis: A new paradigm to explain arousal pathology. In S. Fisher & J. Reason (Eds.), *Handbook of life stress, cognition and health* (pp. 629–649). New York: John Wiley.

Taris, T. W., Kompier, M. A. J., de Lange, A. H., Schaufeli, W., & Schreurs, P. J. G. (2003). Learning new behaviour patterns: A longitudinal test of Karasek's active learning hypothesis among Dutch Teachers. *Work and Stress*, 17, 1–20.

Theorell, T., Ahlberg-Hulten, G., Jodko, M., Sigala, F., & Torre, B. (1993). Influence of job strain and emotion on blood pressure in female hospital personnel during work hours. *Scandinavian Journal Work Environment and Health*, 19, 313–318.

Theorell, T., de Faire, U., Johnson, J., Hall, E., Perski, A., & Stewart, W. (1991). Job strain and ambulatory blood pressure profiles. *Scandinavian Journal of Work, Environment and Health, 17,* 380–385.

Ulich, E. (2001). *Arbeitspsychologie [Work psychology]* (5th ed.). Stuttgart, Germany: Poeschel.

Ulich, E., & Wülser, M. (2004). *Gesundheitsmanagement in Unternehmen—Arbeitspsychologische Perspektiven. Reihe Schweizerische Gesellschaft für Organisation und Management (SGO-Stiftung).* Wiesbaden, Germany: Gabler.

Van Diest, R. (1990). Subjective sleep characteristics as coronary risk factors, their association with Type A behaviour and vital exhaustion. *Journal of Psychosomatic Research, 34,* 415–426.

Volpert, W., Oesterreich, R., Gablenz Kolakovic, S., Krogoll, T., & Resch, M. (1983). *Verfahren zur Ermittlung von Regulationserfordernissen in der Arbeitstätigkeit (VERA) (Method for the assessment of regulation requirements of jobs (VERA): Handbook and manual).* Köln, Germany: TÜV Rheinland.

Warr, P. B. (1990). Decision latitude, job demands, and employee well-being. *Work and Stress, 4,* 285–294.

APPENDIX

The 5-point scale "feedback about the quality of own work" has to be rated with:

level 1: No feedback about the quality of own work is provided.

level 2: Feedback about the quality of own work is less detailed, and/or only given indirectly by deduction from the wages or extra pay. Thus, feedback can not be used constructively.

level 3: Feedback about the quality is delayed or provided too late. Thus, effectiveness of feedbacks is limited or none.

level 4: Feedback about the quality of own work is given immediately, but very generally.

level 5: Feedback about the quality is given immediately, and/or workers can inform themselves actively. Feedback regarding type, cause, and frequency of errors.

EUROPEAN JOURNAL OF WORK AND
ORGANIZATIONAL PSYCHOLOGY
2006, 15 (2), 181–196

Job strain, work rumination, and sleep in school teachers

Mark Cropley

Department of Psychology, School of Human Sciences, University of Surrey, Guildford, UK

Derk-Jan Dijk and Neil Stanley

Surrey Sleep Research Centre, School of Biomedical and Molecular Sciences, University of Surrey, Guildford, UK

The objectives of this study were, firstly, to examine the association between job strain and sleep quality in a sample of primary and secondary school teachers and, secondly, to assess whether the relationship between job strain and sleep quality is mediated or moderated by an individual's inability to "switch-off" from work-related issues during leisure time. School teachers ($N = 143$) completed an hourly record of their work-related thoughts over a workday evening between 5 p.m. and bedtime, and then rated their sleep quality the following morning. Individuals were classified as reporting high ($n = 46$) or low ($n = 52$) job strain using predetermined cut-off scores. Consistent with previous research, the results showed that both groups demonstrated a degree of unwinding and disengagement from work issues over the evening. However, compared to the low job strain group, the high job strain teachers took longer to unwind and ruminated more about work-related issues, over the whole evening, including bedtime. There was no difference in total sleep time between the groups, but high job strain individuals reported poorer sleep quality compared to low job strain individuals. With respect to the second objective, across the whole sample ($N = 143$), work rumination and job strain were significantly correlated with sleep quality, but work rumination was not found to mediate, or moderate the relationship between job strain and sleep quality. It was speculated that the initial low contribution of job strain to sleep quality ($r = -.18$) may have contributed to this null finding. The current findings may have implications for how we assess and manage sleep disturbance in stressed workers.

Correspondence should be addressed to Dr Mark Cropley, Department of Psychology, School of Human Sciences, University of Surrey, Guildford, Surrey GU2 7XH, UK. E-mail: mark.cropley@surrey.ac.uk

© 2006 Psychology Press Ltd

http://www.psypress.com/ejwop   DOI: 10.1080/13594320500513913

One of the most influential occupational theories over the last two decades has been the Job Strain model as formulated by Karasek and Theorell (1990). They suggest that health risks are greater among people who experience high job demands, coupled with low control over how the work is conducted. Demanding jobs, accompanied with low decision latitude, have been associated with a range of physical and psychological stress related disorders (Belkic, Landsbergis, Schnall, & Baker, 2004; Cropley, Steptoe, & Joekes, 1999; Stansfeld, North, White, & Marmot, 1995). Occupational induced stress can often spill over into nonwork time and high job strain individuals in particular have been found to demonstrate delayed psychological and physiological recovery following work (Cropley & Millward Purvis, 2003; Rau, Georgiades, Fredrikson, Lemne, & de Faire, 2001; Steptoe, Cropley, & Joekes, 1999). In one study, for example, Steptoe et al. (1999) investigated the association between cardiovascular disease risk and job strain in a sample of primary and secondary school teachers. The teachers had their blood pressure (BP) monitored over the working day and evening, and readings were accompanied with diary ratings of personal control and stress. It was found that there were no significant differences in BP over the working day between the job strain groups; however, BP decreased to a greater extent in the evening in the low job strain group. The results were not attributable to posture, age, sex, or body mass index.

The mechanism by which high job strain contributed to sustained evening arousal in this study was not ascertained. However, Cropley and Millward Purvis (2003) recently speculated that high job strain individuals may take longer to physiologically unwind following a day's work because they fail to cognitively "switch off" after work, and engage in more ruminative thinking about work-related issues once paid work is completed. In order to test this hypothesis, school teachers were asked to complete a short structured diary about their work-related thoughts from 5 p.m. until 9 p.m. The findings revealed that both high and low job strain workers showed a certain degree of unwinding and disengagement from work-related thoughts during the evening, yet high job strain workers nevertheless took longer to unwind and ruminated more about work-related issues, relative to their low job strain colleagues. These findings were independent of work patterns during the evening. A limitation to this study, however, was that no outcome variable was measured, so it is not clear what role work rumination plays in the path between job strain and well-being.

The present study was designed to replicate and extend this research in two ways. Firstly, we examined the mechanisms by means of which work rumination contributes to sustained cognitive arousal by extending the time frame in which work rumination is measured. We did this by assessing work ruminative thoughts in high and low job strain workers across the whole evening, until bedtime. Secondly, we wished to examine the association between work rumination and sleep quality and in particular whether work rumination mediates or moderates the relationship between job strain and sleep.

There are many conceptualizations of rumination. According to Martin and Tesser (1989), rumination is a generic term which covers a wide range of perseverative thinking. Such thinking, they argue, is characterized: (1) by its frequency, (2) as involving automatic and controlled processing, and (3) for hindering goal attainment. Rumination has been associated with different psychological states including: depression (Nolen-Hoeksema, 1991), anxiety (Mellings & Alden, 2000), anger (Hogan & Linden, 2004; Rusting & Nolen-Hoeksema, 1998), and negative affect (Thomsen et al., 2004). Rumination has also been associated with poor physical health (Thomsen et al., 2004), although the exact role rumination plays in the development and/or progression of physical and psychological disorders is yet to be determined.

There is much evidence to suggest that people tend to ruminate about symptoms of distress or their stressful situations (Lyubomirsky, Tucker, Caldwell, & Berg, 1999; Nolen-Hoeksema, McBride, & Larson, 1997). Alloy and colleagues have recently coined the term "stress-reactive rumination" to describe the type of thinking that occurs following the exposure to stressful life experiences (Alloy et al., 2000; Robinson & Alloy, 2003), and ruminating individuals have been shown to display slower physical recovery after working on a stressful task (Roger & Jamieson, 1988).

Coping responses are known to affect the relationship between stress and well-being (Steptoe, 1991) and rumination has also been conceptualized as a maladaptive coping response (Higgins & Endler, 1995; Papageorgiou & Wells, 2004; Thomsen et al., 2004). According to Lazarus and Folkman (1984), coping can be divided into two broard categories: problem-focused coping and emotion-focused coping. In response to a stressor, a problem-focused approach involves taking direct action, the goal being to reduce either the stressor or enhance resources necessary to deal with it effectively. On the other hand, emotion-focused coping aims to regulate or reduce the emotional consequence of the stressor. In response to a stressor, an individual using an emotion-focusing approach might try to control their feelings by distracting attention away from the stressor, using wishful thinking, or they might cognitively reevaluate their situation. In line with previous conceptualizations, rumination in the present study is considered to be an emotional-focused coping response (Higgins & Endler, 1995; Thomsen et al., 2004).

Sleep is one of the most important recovery mechanisms available to humans, allowing for recovery from daily strains, and therefore a prerequisite for optimal daily functioning and health. The literature suggests that sleep must be continuous for it to be restorative (Walsh & Lindblom, 2000), and sleep loss and sleep disturbance lead to performance decrements, fatigue, mood changes, and immune function impairment (Harrison & Horne, 1999; Rogers, Szuba, Staab, Evans, & Dinges, 2001). Even moderate sleep loss is associated with deficits in alertness and performance (Dinges et al., 1997; Jewett, Dijk, Kronauer, & Dinges, 1999). Although there are many paths to insomnia, there appears to be a degree of consensus within the sleep literature that intrusive cognitions may contribute to sleep disturbance. For example, cognitive arousal at bedtime appears to be linked with insomnia (Gross & Borkovec, 1982; Harvey, 2000), and work-related worries appear to contribute to self-reported sleep disturbance (Åkerstedt et al., 2002). Studies that have specifically examined rumination and insomnia have found a relationship between rumination and sleep quality in both healthy individuals (Thomsen, Mehlsen, Christensen, & Zachariae, 2003) and psychiatric patients (Bertelson & Monroe, 1979; Kales, Caldwell, Soldatos, Bixler, & Kales, 1983). Thus, there is strong evidence that cognitive arousal at bedtime is associated with increased sleep disturbance.

Coping resources have been found to mediate and moderate the link between stress and sleep (Åkerstedt et al., 2002; Sadeh, Keinan, & Daon, 2004), so it is probable that work rumination would both mediate and moderate the relationship between job strain and sleep. A mediation variable is one which intervenes or accounts for the relationship between a predictor variable and an outcome variable. Mediation is a hypothesized causal chain where one variable affects another variable, that turn affects a third variable. By contrast, a moderating variable is a third variable that affects the direction and/or strength of the relationship between two other variables (Baron & Kenny, 1986).

The theoretical link between job strain, rumination, and sleep was examined in the present study within a population of school teachers. School teaching is considered to be a high stress occupation (Travers & Cooper, 1996) involving high commitment, and school teachers have been shown to find it difficult to recuperate after work (Aronsson, Svensson, & Gustafsson, 2003), and to be distracted by work issues when at home (Cardenas, Major, & Bernas, 2004). Compared to the general population, teachers with high job strain have also been found to report poorer sleep (Cropley et al., 1999). In the present study individuals were instructed to complete a structured rumination and sleep diary, which assessed work ruminative thoughts over a workday evening, and self-reported sleep the following morning. It was predicted that relative to low job strain, high job strain individuals would take longer to unwind following work, and would ruminate more about work issues over the evening up to bedtime (Hypothesis 1). As coping resources have been found to mediate and moderate the link between stress and sleep (Åkerstedt et al., 2002; Sadeh et al., 2004), it was also predicted that work rumination would both mediate and moderate the relationship between job strain and sleep (Hypothesis 2).

METHOD

Participants

Participants were recruited from primary and secondary schools in Surrey, UK. Each school was initially contacted by letter explaining the nature of the study, and a member of the research team gave a short presentation to those teachers interested in participating. Individuals who volunteered, and were full-time, were given an information pack together with the diary and a freepost return envelope. A total of 170 diaries were distributed, and 151 were returned by the specified deadline, amounting to a response rate of 88.8%. Five diaries were excluded because participants reported being disturbed by external factors whilst sleeping (e.g., awoken by a child or a phone call), or they reported taking sleep medication. A further three diaries were excluded because of incomplete information. The final sample consisted of 143 teachers whose age ranged from 21 to 59 years, with a mean of 38.61 years ($SD = 11.23$ years). The majority of the sample (74%) worked in primary schools and the remaining 26% were from secondary schools. They had been working in the teaching profession from 3 months to 34 years (mean 13.0 years). The sample was predominately female (83.2%). Ninety-four (65.7%) participants were married or living with their partner, nine (6.3%) were separated, divorced, or widowed, and forty (28%) were single.

Materials

Job strain.   Job strain was assessed using a 10-item self-report measure adapted from Karasek and Theorell (1990). Three items concern perceived job control (e.g., "I have freedom to decide what I do in my job"), three items concern job demands (e.g., "The pace of work in my job is very intense"), and four items refer to skill utilization (e.g., "My job involves me learning new things"). Participants rate each statement along a 4-point scale ranging from 1 ("strongly disagree") to 4 ("strongly agree"). The job strain score is computed as job strain = job demand/(job control + skill utilization). The validity of this measure has been demonstrated in a number of previous studies (e.g., Cropley & Millward Purvis, 2003; Evans & Steptoe, 2001, 2002; Steptoe et al., 1999). Classification of high and low job strain teachers followed Steptoe et al. (1999): high job strain above 13.3 (men) and 13.5 (women); and low job strain below 11.3 (men) and 12.4 (women). The internal consistency (Cronbach's α) for this measure was .75.

Work rumination/sleep diary and procedure.   The work rumination and sleep questions were incorporated into a small diary that was completed over one workday evening and the following morning. Four work rumination questions were used: (1) "Did you think about work in the last hour?" (2) "Did you think about future work, e.g., lessons, tomorrow?" (3) "Did you think about things that had happened at work today or before today?" (4) "Would you describe your thoughts in the last hour as repetitive/recurring?" Each was rated on a 7-point scale ranging from 1 ("not at all") to 7 ("all the time"). These questions are similar to those used by Cropley and Millward Purvis (2003). Participants were required to indicate their choice by circling an appropriate number. Each double-page entry contained information relating to 1 hour. Additional questions sought information about location, posture, and activity. Ratings were made hourly from 5 p.m. until bedtime, and the data from the four rumination questions were averaged for each time point. The internal consistency (Cronbach's α) of the rumination scale over the evening was good: 5 p.m. = .78, 6 p.m. = .79, 7 p.m. = .84, 8 p.m. = .85, 9 p.m. = .86, 10 p.m. = .86, bedtime = .88.

Upon awakening, participants reported how long they had slept and whether they had been purposefully woken during the night, e.g., because of childcare duties or telephone calls, etc. They also answered a series of sleep quality questions: "Did you sleep throughout the night?" "Was it difficult or easy to fall asleep?" "Did you wake up early?" "Did you wake up easily?" "Did you dream?" "How refreshed did you feel in morning upon waking?" "How well did you sleep?" and "Was your sleep restless or calm?" These questions were rated on a 7-point scale with the lower number indicating poorer sleep. For example, "Was it difficult or easy to fall asleep?" was rated from 1 ("very difficult") to 7 ("very easy"). Similar items have been used in previous sleep research (Åkerstedt, Hume, Minors, & Waterhouse, 1994). Factor analysis was carried out on the eight sleep quality questions. Three factors emerged with Eigenvalues greater than one, together accounting for 70.5% of the variance. A varimax rotation was performed; variables were loaded on a single factor on the basis of the highest score. Items with a loading greater than 0.4 were retained. The first factor contained five items (did you sleep throughout the night, did you wake up early, difficult or easy to fall asleep, how well did you sleep, and was your sleep restless or calm), had an Eigenvalue of 3.4 and accounted for 42% of the variance. The internal consistency (Cronbach's α) of this factor was good, .79, and the factor was labelled sleep quality. The second factor consisting of two items (wake up easily, and how refreshed were you after awakening) had an Eigenvalue of 1.3, and accounted for 16% of the variance and the third factor (any dreams) accounted for 12.5%, and had an Eigenvalue of 1, but contained only one item. As the second two factors contained only two items and one item respectively, they were excluded from further analyses.

Data analysis

The main analyses are divided into three sections. The first section compares data from the high and low job strain groups on work rumination over the evening from 5 p.m. to bedtime. The effect of job strain on work rumination was analysed using a Group (high/low job strain) × Time (5 p.m., 6 p.m., 7 p.m., 8 p.m., 9 p.m., 10 p.m., bedtime), repeated measures ANOVA. Mean comparisons were computed using planned t-tests. The second set of analyses included the participants with intermediate ratings of job strain scores and reports correlations of demographic characteristics, work measures, work rumination, and sleep ($N = 143$). Tests for mediation and moderation are presented in the third section. Work ruminative data for the hour preceding bedtime is used in this analysis. Three participants in the low job strain group and three in the high job strain group reported working in the hour preceding sleep. However, their data were left in this analysis, as omitting them made no difference to the overall pattern of results. Baron and Kenny (1986) proposed a four-step process for testing mediation. To test whether work rumination mediates the relationship between job strain and sleep quality, for example, the following four regression equations need to be performed: (1) Job strain should be related to sleep quality, (2) job strain should also be related to work rumination, and (3) rumination should be related to sleep quality; in the fourth step, a regression equation is performed with both job strain and rumination entered to predict sleep quality. If rumination, but not job strain, continues to affect sleep quality, this is consistent with a full mediation model. If rumination continues to affect sleep quality, after controlling for the direct effects of job strain, but job strain continues to be associated with sleep quality (albeit with reduced variance) this is consistent with a partial mediation model. By contrast, a moderating variable, as stated in the introduction, is a third variable which affects the relationship between two other variables. The underlying assumption here is that the effect of an independent variable on a dependent variable will be reliant on the second independent variable or moderator. In practice, a moderating model is supported if the interaction between two variables is significantly associated with a predictor variable (Baron & Kenny, 1986).

RESULTS

Ninety-eight individuals were categorized into the high ($n = 46$) and low job strain ($n = 52$) groups. The characteristics of the participants and questionnaire data are summarized and presented in Table 1. There were no significant differences between the groups with respect to sex, age, teaching experience, or the number of hours worked at home during the

TABLE 1
Participants' characteristics in the low and high job strain groups

	Low job strain (n = 52)	High job strain (n = 46)
Sex		
Male	5	7
Female	47	39
Age (years)	38.1 (12.1)	42.2 (10.3)
School type (%)		
Primary	75	72
Secondary	25	28
Years of teaching	12.6 (11.0)	16.3 (10.7)
Minutes worked at home that evening	72.6 (60.9)	93.9 (82.6)
Total sleep time (hrs/min)	6.41 (0.9)	6.28 (1.0)
Sleep quality	5.1 (1.2)	4.3 (1.4)**
Job strain	10.4 (1.5)	15.4 (1.8)**

Standard deviation in parenthesis.
$*p < .05$, $**p < .001$ difference between groups.

evening of testing. The average reported sleep time was 6 hours and 48 minutes. There were no significant differences between the groups in reported sleep time, but high job strain teachers reported poorer sleep, relative to low job strain teachers. Consistent with the gender ratio of school teachers in the UK, there were more females than males in each group. By design there was a significant difference in job strain between the high/low job strain groups.

Ruminative thought

Ratings of work rumination over the workday evening revealed a significant main effect of group, $F(1, 96) = 7.13$, $p < .01$, and time, $F(6, 96) = 82.3$, $p < .001$, but there was no significant Group × Time interaction, $F(1, 96) = 1.23$, ns. These means are shown in Figure 1. Compared to ratings made at 5 p.m., work rumination was significantly lower at 6 p.m., 7 p.m., 8 p.m., 9 p.m., 10 p.m., and bedtime (all $ps < .001$). Ratings of work rumination at bedtime were significantly lower compared to those made at 6 p.m., 7 p.m., 8 p.m., 9 p.m. and 10 p.m. (all $ps < .05$). Overall, these results demonstrate that work rumination was greatest early in the evening but then declined thereafter until bedtime.

Correlational analyses

For the correlational analyses all the variables were treated as continuous and the data from all the participants were used. Neither job strain nor sleep quality was significantly correlated with any of the demographic variables. Work rumination was significantly correlated with marital status; married or living with a partner was associated with reporting less work rumination in the hour preceding bed. Sleep quality was significantly correlated with sleep time; longer sleep time was associated with higher sleep quality. Sex was not significantly correlated with any variable. The complete correlation matrix is presented in Table 2.

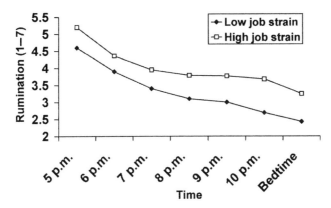

Figure 1.   Rumination about work during the evening from 5 p.m. to bedtime in high and low job strain individuals.

TABLE 2

Bivariate correlations between demographic, work, work rumination at bedtime, and sleep quality variables

	Age	*Sex*	*MStatus*	*YearsT*	*HomeW*	*SleepT*	*JStrain*	*RumB*
Age								
Sex	−.02							
MStatus	−.34**	.08						
YearsT	.84**	−.05	−.31**					
HomeW	.14	−.01	−.17*	.03				
SleepT	−.39**	−.12	.12	−.32**	.03			
JStrain	.06	.07	−.15	.10	.10	−.11		
RumB	.02	−.02	−.20*	.03	.13	−.21**	.18*	
SleepQ	−.07	.06	.13	−.01	.06	.28**	−.18*	−.24**

*$p < .05$; **$p < .01$.

Sex = 1 male, 2 female; MStatus = marital status (1 married or living with partner, 2 single); YearsT = years teaching, HomeW = time working at home during the evening; SleepT = total sleep time, JStrain = job strain, RumB = work rumination at bedtime, SleepQ = sleep quality.

Test for mediation

Consistent with the hypothesized first mediation step, job strain was significantly correlated with sleep ($r = -.18$, $p < .01$) as higher job strain scores were associated with reduced sleep quality. The second step was also supported—job strain was significantly correlated with work rumination in the hour preceding sleep, in the predicted direction, i.e., higher job strain scores were associated with greater rumination, $r = .18$, $p < .05$. Work rumination was also significantly associated with reduced sleep quality supporting Step 3, $r = -.24$, $p < .001$. In the fourth and crucial last step, job strain failed to significantly predict sleep quality once the variance associated with rumination was controlled, $\beta = -.15$, $t = -1.71$, $p = .08$, although work rumination continued to be significantly associated with sleep quality after controlling for the variance associated with job strain, $\beta = -.21$, $t = -2.65$, $p < .01$. However as the reduction in beta was very small for job strain once work rumination was added to the model (.03), the present, results therefore, do not support our hypothesis that work rumination mediates the path between job strain and sleep quality.

Test for moderation

To test the interaction hypothesis, a hierarchical regression analysis was performed following mean centring and the creation of a multiplicative (cross-product) term (Aiken & West, 1991). This was to eliminate the possibility of multicollinearity between the main effects and the interaction effect on sleep. The order of entry was job strain and work rumination in the hour preceding bed, and then the interaction (Job strain × Work rumination) term. There was a significant main effect of job strain, $\beta = -.18$, $t = -2.28$, $p < .05$, and a significant main effect of work rumination, $\beta = -.21$, $t = -2.13$, $p < .05$, but the Job strain × Work rumination interaction was nonsignificant, $\beta = -.14$, $t = -1.42$, ns. Thus the effect of job strain on sleep quality was not moderated by work rumination.

DISCUSSION

The main objective of this study was to examine the relationship between job strain, work rumination, and subjective sleep in a population of school teachers. Consistent with the previous findings of Cropley and Millward Purvis (2003), and Hypothesis 1, work rumination was higher in the early evening and declined as the evening progressed as individuals gradually unwound and relaxed. Also as expected, high job strain teachers, demonstrated a greater likelihood of ruminative thinking, across the whole evening, relative to low job strain teachers. This finding could not be explained by work patterns as there was no difference between the groups in the time spent on school work over the evening. Given that teaching is regarded as a high stress occupation (Travers & Cooper, 1996), it is perhaps not surprising that some teachers failed to successfully "switch off" and disengage from work-related issues during their leisure time. Unlike previous research, however, there was no interaction between job strain and work rumination.

Workers in demanding jobs frequently complain of sleep disturbance and many attribute this to thinking about work-related thoughts at bedtime and during the night (Kecklund & Åkerstedt, 2004). In the present study we predicted that ruminating about work issues in the hour preceding bedtime would be associated with greater sleep disturbance. This expectation was supported: Job strain and work rumination were negatively associated with sleep quality. However, against expectations (Hypothesis 2), work rumination did not mediate or moderate the relationship between job strain and sleep quality in the present study. Unfortunately, the initial path between job strain and sleep quality was relatively low at $r = -.18$, and once work rumination was added to the model, the beta value was only reduced by a very small amount, .03. One possible reason for this could be the job strain measure used in the study. The job strain measure was more of a trait questionnaire, seeking information about perceptions of the working environment in general, and future research may find a stronger correlation with sleep quality if a state or specific measure of job strain is used that seeks information about how stressful the job was that day. In many occupations, including the teaching profession, job demands fluctuate on a daily basis, with some days being more stressful and demanding than others. It follows that sleep disturbance would be more likely on those days that were particularly demanding or stressful, for instance when there has been a conflict or other kind of problem, and less likely on stress-free days.

Interestingly there was no difference in reported sleep time between the high and low job strain teachers. The mean sleep length was 6 hours and 38 minutes. This figure is lower than reported nationally (Groeger, Zijlstra, & Dijk, 2004), and indicates that many teachers have restrictive sleep—at least within the working week. It is possible that some teachers compensate and make up for lost sleep at the weekend, although, at the moment, this is speculative. Care, however, should be exercised in the interpretation of this result until it is qualified by more objective measures, and future research could try to validate the findings by using more objective sleep measures such as sleep actigraphy (Stanley, 2003), or sleep polysomnography. A recent study found a reduction of slow wave sleep (SWS) in working individuals who were apprehensive about their work the following day (Kecklund & Åkerstedt, 2004).

We assume that ruminating about work issues in the hour before bed raises cognitive and physiological arousal of the central nervous system, and being highly aroused delays sleep onset and leads to poorer sleep. Laboratory studies have shown that individuals who ruminate following the completion of a challenging task tend to show prolonged physiological arousal (Roger & Jamieson, 1988), and being aroused at bedtime delays sleep onset (Gross & Borkovec, 1982; Harvey, 2000; Harvey & Payne, 2002). The present findings are consistent with this work. Unfortunately, it was not possible to take physiological readings in the above study, so the link between rumination and autonomic arousal on sleep quality could not be established. It will be of theoretical interest to validate the rumination questions against physiological measures by showing higher ruminative thinking to be associated with high levels of arousal. Conversely reducing or blocking ruminative thought should result in lower arousal and improved sleep quality.

Although not one of the major objectives, we also examined the role of sex with respect to work rumination. It was interesting that sex was not significantly correlated with rumination. Nolen-Hoeksema (1987), in her work on depressive rumination, found women to show more ruminative thinking then men. It has been speculated that one reason for this is because women face different sources of stressors compared to men. Women have also been shown to become more distressed over home/family demands, while men become distressed over work matters (Almeida & Kessler, 1998; Conger, Lorenz, Elder, Simons, & Ge, 1993). It is not clear why there was no difference between men and women with regards to their ruminative responses in the present study, although one possibility is that because they came from a single occupation group, they experience similar stresses and strains—particularly at work. However, caution needs to be exercised here, as there were fewer men in the study and this could have been the main reason for not finding sex differences.

It is not only those individuals who experience high job strain who may think about work issues during free time. People who perceive their jobs as rewarding, stimulating, and challenging may also find themselves thinking about work issues during their leisure time. Indeed, repeatedly thinking about a certain area of work may be welcomed by some, as it will help them stay focused on the task at hand. Although such ways of thinking may appear effectual, particularly in the short term, the continual emphasis on work at the cost of not attending to "other spheres of life" may eventually lead to stress (Griffith, Steptoe, & Cropley, 1999). The rumination questions in the present study sought information only about work-related thoughts but no distinction was made concerning whether these thoughts were voluntary/involuntary or intrusive. Here rumination was considered as a form of cognitive arousal; the emotionality of the thoughts was not assessed. Negative presleep cognitive activity has been associated with certain sleep parameters in some studies (Harvey, 2000). In order to extend our understanding of these issues, further research is needed to examine not only the level of cognitive activity at bedtime but also the emotional content and the level of control an individual has over such thoughts. A greater understanding of these issues is needed as this will aid interventions aimed at improving sleep quality in stressed workers.

A potential problem with using pen and pencil diaries is that researchers can never be certain that study participants completed the questions at the times requested, and this could be a limitation with the present study. It was reassuring that the results mirrored an earlier study (Cropley & Millward Purvis, 2003); however, future work could use electronic diaries to record the exact time entries are made to address this issue. There are other limitations of this study that warrant discussion. The present results are essentially correlational. Demonstrating an association between work rumination and sleep quality does not mean that rumination about work issues causes sleep problems. Poor sleep could affect one's perceptions of work or lower work performance, leading people to ruminate about work issues during their leisure time. To demonstrate causality, an experiment is required where manipulations of work ruminative thinking produce variations in sleep quality. Another limitation concerns other factors that could possibly affect sleep. It is well known that sleep can be disrupted by a number of *sleep-interfering* factors like caffeine intake, light, noise, and stressful life events (excluding work) and none of those variables were measured in the present study. In order to keep the diary short and not to overburden participants it was impractical to measure all the factors that are known to effect sleep. The very fact that sleep quality was associated with work rumination, despite not controlling for these other factors, demonstrates how pervasive the relationship between work rumination and sleep is.

Finally, this study was performed with school teachers and school teaching is a high commitment occupation (Aronsson et al., 2003), so it is not known whether the results will generalize to other occupational groups. Relative to many occupations, school teachers are thought to work long hours at home, and are distracted by work-related issues while at home (Cardenas et al., 2004), and therefore have less time to recover and unwind. There are, however, no logical reasons why the results should not generalize, especially in other professional groups of workers, e.g., accountants, health practitioners, or the police, or in occupations where there are blurred boundaries between home and work. Further research with other occupational groups is undoubtedly needed.

The validity of these findings ultimately depends on their representativeness. The measurement of work rumination may be seen as being problematic as it may implicitly encourage introspective thought. The question therefore arises: Do people behave or sleep as "normal" at night after completing a diary assessment that prompts them to think about work issues? We do not know the answer to this question, but 71% of the sample rated their sleep as typical for that night.

In conclusion, this study has demonstrated that ruminative thinking about work issues at bedtime can predict perceptions of sleep quality. These results suggest that suitable methods aimed at disrupting, reducing, or blocking this style of thinking would result in a better quality of sleep for workers. Future research is needed to ascertain how best to do this. Many teachers take work home and the interface between work and home boundaries is blurred. Working at home does not necessarily translate into poor sleep; how easily one is able to "switch off" once work is completed appears to be the crucial factor predicting good quality sleep.

REFERENCES

Aiken, L. S., & West, S. G. (1991). *Multiple regression: Testing and interpreting interactions.* Newbury Park, CA: Sage.

Åkerstedt, T., Hume, K., Minors, D., & Waterhouse, J. (1994). The meaning of good sleep: A longitudinal study of polysomnography and subjective sleep quality. *Journal of Sleep Research, 3,* 152–158.

Åkerstedt, T., Knutsson, A., Westerholm, P., Theorell, T., Alfredsson, L., & Kecklund, G. (2002). Sleep disturbances, work stress and work hours: A cross-sectional study. *Journal of Psychosomatic Research, 53,* 741–748.

Alloy, L. B., Abramson, L. Y., Hogan, M. E., Whitehouse, W. G., Rose, D. T., Robinson, M. S., et al. (2000). The Temple-Wisconsin Cognitive Vulnerability to Depression Project: Lifetime history of axis I psychopathology in individuals at high and low cognitive risk for depression. *Journal of Abnormal Psychology, 109,* 403–418.

Almeida, D. M., & Kessler, R. C. (1998). Everyday stressors and gender differences in daily distress. *Journal of Personality and Social Psychology, 75,* 670–680.

Aronsson, G., Svensson, L., & Gustafsson, K. (2003). Unwinding, recuperation and health among compulsory-school and high-school school teachers in Sweden. *International Journal of Stress Management, 10,* 217–234.

Baron, R. M., & Kenny, D. A. (1986). The moderator–mediator variable distinction in social psychological research: Conceptual, strategic, and statistical considerations. *Journal of Personality and Social Psychology, 51,* 1173–1182.

Belkic, K. L., Landsbergis, P. A., Schnall, P. L., & Baker, D. (2004). Is job strain a major source of cardiovascular disease risk? *Scandinavian Journal of Work, Environment and Health, 30,* 85–128.

Bertelson, A. D., & Monroe, L. J. (1979). Personality patterns of adolescent poor and good sleepers. *Journal of Abnormal Child Psychology, 7,* 191–197.

Cardenas, R. A., Major, D. A., & Bernas, K. H. (2004). Exploring work and family distractions: Antecedents and outcomes. *International Journal of Stress Management, 11,* 346–365.

Conger, R. D., Lorenz, F. O., Elder, G. H., Jr., Simons, R. L., & Ge, X. (1993). Husband and wife differences in response to undesirable life events. *Journal of Health and Social Behavior, 34,* 71–88.

Cropley, M., & Millward Purvis, L. J. (2003). Job strain and rumination about work issues during leisure time: A diary study. *European Journal of Work and Organizational Psychology, 12,* 195–207.

Cropley, M., Steptoe, A., & Joekes, K. (1999). Job strain and psychiatric morbidity. *Psychological Medicine, 29*, 1411–1416.

Dinges, D. F., Pack, F., Williams, K., Gillen, K. A., Powell, J. W., Ott, G. E., et al. (1997). Cumulative sleepiness, mood disturbance, and psychomotor vigilance performance decrements during a week of sleep restricted to 4–5 hours per night. *Sleep, 20*, 267–277.

Evans, O., & Steptoe, A. (2001). Social support at work, heart rate, and cortisol: A self-monitoring study. *Journal of Occupational Health Psychology, 6*, 361–370.

Evans, O., & Steptoe, A. (2002). The contribution of gender-role orientation, work factors and home stressors to psychological well-being and sickness absence in male- and female-dominated occupational groups. *Social Science and Medicine, 54*, 481–492.

Griffith, J., Steptoe, A., & Cropley, M. (1999). An investigation of coping strategies associated with job stress in teachers. *British Journal of Educational Psychology, 69*, 517–531.

Groeger, J. A., Zijlstra, F. R. H., & Dijk, D.-J. (2004). Sleep quantity, sleep difficulties and their perceived consequences in a representative sample of some 2000 British adults. *Journal of Sleep Research, 13*, 359–371.

Gross, R. T., & Borkovec, T. D. (1982). The effects of a cognitive intrusion manipulation on the sleep-onset latency of good sleepers. *Behaviour Therapy, 13*, 112–116.

Harrison, Y., & Horne, J. A. (1999). One night of sleep loss impairs innovative thinking and flexible decision making. *Organizational Behaviour and Human Decision Processes, 78*, 128–145.

Harvey, A. G. (2000). Pre-sleep cognitive activity: A comparison of sleep-onset insomniacs and good sleepers. *British Journal of Clinical Psychology, 39*, 275–286.

Harvey, A. G., & Payne, S. (2002). The management of unwanted pre-sleep thoughts in insomnia: Distraction with imagery versus general distraction. *Behavior Research and Therapy, 40*, 267–277.

Higgins, J. E., & Endler, N. S. (1995). Coping, life stress, and psychological and somatic distress. *European Journal of Personality, 9*, 253–270.

Hogan, B. E., & Linden, W. (2004). Anger response styles and blood pressure: At least don't ruminate about it! *Annals of Behavioral Medicine, 27*, 38–49.

Jewett, M. E., Dijk, D.-J., Kronauer, R. E., & Dinges, D. F. (1999). Dose-response relationship between sleep duration and human psychomotor vigilance and subjective alertness. *Sleep, 15*, 171–179.

Kales, A., Caldwell, A. B., Soldatos, C. R., Bixler, E. O., & Kales, J. D. (1983). Biopsychobehavioral correlates of insomnia: II. Pattern specificity and consistency with the Minnesota Multiphasic Personality Inventory. *Psychosomatic Medicine, 45*, 341–356.

Karasek, R. A., & Theorell, T. (1990). *Healthy work*. New York: Basic Books.

Kecklund, G., & Åkerstedt, T. (2004). Apprehension of the subsequent working day is associated with a low amount of slow wave sleep. *Biological Psychology, 66*, 169–176.

Lazarus, R. S., & Folkman, S. (1984). *Stress, appraisal, and coping*. New York: Springer.

Lyubomirsky, S., Tucker, K. L., Caldwell, N. D., & Berg, K. (1999). Why ruminators are poor problem solvers: Clues from the phenomenology of dysphoric rumination. *Journal of Personality and Social Psychology, 77*, 1041–1060.

Martin, L. L., & Tesser, A. (1989). Toward a motivational and structural theory of ruminative thought. In J. Uleman & J. A. Bargh (Eds.), *Unintended thought* (pp. 306–326). New York: Guilford Press.

Mellings, T. M. B., & Alden, L. E. (2000). Cognitive processes in social anxiety: The effects of self-focus, rumination and anticipatory processing. *Behaviour Research and Therapy, 38*, 243–257.

Nolen-Hoeksema, S. (1987). Sex differences in unipolar depression: Evidence and theory. *Psychological Bulletin, 101*, 259–282.

Nolen-Hoeksema, S. (1991). Responses to depression and their effects on the duration of depressive episodes [Review]. *Journal of Abnormal Psychology, 100*, 569–582.

Nolen-Hoeksema, S., McBride, A., & Larson, J. (1997). Rumination and psychological distress among bereaved partners. *Journal of Personality and Social Psychology, 72*, 855–862.

Papageorgiou, C., & Wells, A. (2004). Nature, functions, and beliefs about depressive rumination. In C. Papageorgiou & A. Wells (Eds.), *Depressive rumination: Nature, theory and treatment* (pp. 3–20). New York: Wiley.

Rau, R., Georgiades, A., Fredrikson, M., Lemne, C., & de Faire, U. (2001). Psychosocial work characteristics and perceived control in relation to cardiovascular rewind at night. *Journal of Occupational Health Psychology, 6*, 171–181.

Robinson, M. S., & Alloy, L. B. (2003). Negative cognitive styles and stress-reactive rumination interact to predict depression: A prospective study. *Cognitive Therapy and Research, 27*, 275–291.

Roger, D., & Jamieson, J. (1988). Individual differences in delayed heart-rate recovery following stress: The role of extraversion, neuroticism and emotional control. *Personality and Individual Differences, 9*, 721–726.

Rogers, N. L., Szuba, M. P., Staab, J. P., Evans, D. L., & Dinges, D. F. (2001). Neuroimmunologic aspects of sleep and sleep loss. *Seminars in Clinical Neuropsychiatry, 6*, 295–307.

Rusting, C. L., & Nolen-Hoeksema, S. (1998). Regulating responses to anger: Effects of rumination and distraction on angry mood. *Journal of Personality and Social Psychology, 74*, 790–803.

Sadeh, A., Keinan, G., & Daon, K. (2004). Effects of stress on sleep: The moderating role of coping style. *Health Psychology, 23*, 542–545.

Stanley, N. (2003). Actigraphy in human psychopharmacology: A review. *Human Psychopharmacology, 18*, 39–49.

Stansfeld, S. A., North, F. M., White, I., & Marmot, M. G. (1995). Work characteristics and psychiatric disorder in civil servants in London. *Journal of Epidemiology and Community Health, 49*, 48–53.

Steptoe, A. (1991). Invited review: The links between stress and illness. *Journal of Psychosomatic Research, 35*, 633–644.

Steptoe, A., Cropley, M., & Joekes, K. (1999). Job strain, blood pressure, and response to uncontrollable stress. *Journal of Hypertension, 17*, 193–200.

Thomsen, D. K., Mehlsen, Y. M., Christensen S., & Zachariae, R. (2003). Rumination—relationship with negative mood and sleep quality. *Personality and Individual Differences, 34*, 1293–1301.

Thomsen, D. K., Mehlsen, M. Y., Olesen, F., Hokland, M., Viidik, A., Avlund, K., & Zachariae, R. (2004). Is there an association between rumination and self-reported physical health? A one-year follow-up in a young and an elderly sample. *Journal of Behavioural Medicine, 27*, 215–231.

Travers, C. J., & Cooper, C. L. (1996). *Teachers under pressure: Stress in the teaching profession.* London: Routledge.

Walsh, J. K., & Lindblom, S. S. (2000). Psychophysiology of sleep deprivation and disruption. In M. R. Pressman & W. C. Orr. (Eds.), *Understanding sleep: The evaluation and treatment of sleep disorders* (pp. 73–110). Washington, DC: APA.

EUROPEAN JOURNAL OF WORK AND
ORGANIZATIONAL PSYCHOLOGY
2006, 15 (2), 197–217

Psychological detachment from work during off-job time: The role of job stressors, job involvement, and recovery-related self-efficacy

Sabine Sonnentag

Department of Psychology, University of Konstanz, Konstanz, Germany

Undine Kruel

Institute of Psychology, Technical University of Braunschweig, Braunschweig, Germany

Previous research has suggested that psychological detachment from work during off-job time is important in order to recover from stress encountered at the job. Psychological detachment refers to an individual's experience of being mentally away from work, to make a pause in thinking about work-related issues, thus to "switch off". This study examines job stressors, job involvement, and recovery-related self-efficacy as predictors of psychological detachment in a sample of 148 school teachers. Psychological detachment was assessed by self-reports and by ratings provided by family members. Multiple regression analysis showed that workload, job involvement, and recovery-related self-efficacy were significant predictors of both self-rated and family-rated psychological detachment. The study findings suggest that with respect to practical implications it is crucial to manage workload and to increase recovery-related self-efficacy.

Research has shown that stressors encountered at the job have a negative effect on employees' mental and physical health (cf. for reviews, de Lange, Taris, Kompier, Houtman, & Bongers, 2003; Kahn & Byosiere, 1992; Sonnentag & Frese, 2003). Particularly during the past decade researchers became increasingly interested in the question of how employees use their off-job time to recover and unwind from stressful work. This research

Correspondence should be addressed to Sabine Sonnentag, Department of Psychology, University of Konstanz, Postbox D42, D-78457 Konstanz, Germany.
E-mail: sabine.sonnentag@uni-konstanz.de
We are grateful to Charlotte Fritz, Sandra Ohly, Saskia Weh, and anonymous reviewers for very helpful comments on earlier versions of this article.

http://www.psypress.com/ejwop   DOI: 10.1080/13594320500513939

addressed both relatively long off-job time periods such as vacations and relatively short periods such as free evenings during normal work weeks (cf. for reviews, Eden, 2001a, 2001b).

These studies on recovery processes showed that employee well-being improves during off-job time (Strauss-Blasche, Ekmekcioglu, & Marktl, 2000; Westman & Eden, 1997; Westman & Etzion, 2001). Moreover, recovery experiences were found to be positively related to subsequent on-the-job behaviour (Sonnentag, 2003). In addition, studies illustrated that recovery issues are closely linked to features of the work situation. Particularly, employees who face highly stressful work situations express a high need for recovery (Sluiter, Frings-Dresen, van der Beek, & Meijman, 2001; Sluiter, van der Beek, & Frings-Dresen, 1999; Sonnentag & Zijlstra, in press). This high need for recovery is experienced as the desire for being—temporarily—relieved from demands in order to replenish one's resources.

Research suggests that psychological detachment from work during off-job time is highly relevant for recovery to occur (Etzion, Eden, & Lapidot, 1998; Sonnentag & Bayer, 2005). Individual well-being benefits more from off-job time when individuals are able to mentally "switch off". Until now, predictors of psychological detachment from work have not been examined systematically. However, first studies suggest that job stressors and high job strain situations make it difficult to detach from work during off-job time (Cropley & Millward Purvis, 2003; Grebner, Semmer, & Elfering, 2005; Sonnentag & Bayer, 2005). Other factors including individual difference variables that might also be relevant for psychological detachment were largely neglected in previous studies. In our study, we aim at a more comprehensive examination of predictors of psychological detachment. Specifically, we will focus on a broader range of job stressors, as well as job involvement, and recovery-related self-efficacy.

THE DETACHMENT CONCEPT

One experience that is important for recovery to occur is psychological detachment from work during off-job time. Etzion et al. (1998) referred to psychological detachment as "sense of detachment from work routine" and defined it as "the individual's sense of being away from the work situation" (p. 579). It is important to note that psychological detachment is more than just being physically away from the workplace. Psychological detachment implies that one is not occupied by work-related duties. For example, being at home, but making job-related phone calls or completing other job-related tasks, will make psychological detachment impossible. For psychological detachment to occur it is necessary to disengage oneself psychologically from work. This disengagement implies ceasing to think about or ruminate on job-related issues. In every-day terms, psychological detachment from work is often experienced as "switching off" when being away from one's workplace (Sonnentag & Bayer, 2005).

Research has shown that psychological detachment helps in recovering from work stress. For example, Etzion et al. (1998) examined the effect of detachment from one's job during a reserve military service. Analysis showed that during the reserve service burnout and stress decreased. Moreover, individuals who psychologically detached from their jobs during a reserve service that they experienced as "positive" reported greater relief from burnout and stress than those who continued to be closely connected to their jobs. Sonnentag and Bayer (2005) conducted a daily survey study over 3 working days and found that psychological detachment from one's job during leisure activities resulted in a better mood and less fatigue at bedtime than continued thinking about job-related issues—even when controlling for preleisure positive mood and fatigue. Studies that more directly assessed involvement in job-related activities at home resulted in similar findings: The less time individuals spent on job-related activities during the evening, the better was their well-being at bedtime (Sonnentag, 2001; Sonnentag & Zijlstra, in press).

PREDICTORS OF DETACHMENT

Job stressors

We assume that job stressors are negatively related to psychological detachment from work during off-job time. One job stressor that is particularly detrimental to detachment is high workload. High workload implies that one has to accomplish a high amount of work within little time. Workload is often experienced as time pressure. There are several reasons why high workload should be negatively related to detachment: We assume that individuals who face a high amount of work may feel the necessity to take work home and to accomplish job-related tasks at home. When being still busy with job-related tasks, it is impossible to psychologically detach oneself from work. In addition, even when not taking work home or not deliberately working on job-related tasks at home, in case of high workload, it is likely that one has not completed all tasks during the day at work. Therefore, one will tend to continue thinking about these unfinished tasks and about how to complete them during the next days. Moreover, in high workload situations, one will feel strained from work when being at home and one might anticipate high workload for the future days. Therefore, it will be difficult to psychologically detach oneself from work.

Recent diary studies provide some support for the assumed negative relationship between workload and detachment. Cropley and Millward Purvis (2003) examined the degree of rumination about job-related issues among school teachers between 5 p.m. and 9 p.m. At 5 p.m. all teachers showed a relatively high level of rumination. During the course of the evening, teachers in low strain jobs (i.e., jobs with low workload) showed a fast decrement in rumination, indicating that they were successful in psychologically detaching from work. Teachers in high strain jobs (i.e., jobs with high workload), however, showed a less prominent decline in rumination and were still ruminating about their job at 9 p.m. Similarly, in the daily survey study with individuals from different occupations, Sonnentag and Bayer (2005) found negative effects of chronic time pressure and the amount of daily work hours on psychological detachment from work during evening hours.

However, high workload is not the only stressor encountered at the workplace. Role stress theory argues that role ambiguity and role conflict are also relevant stressors in work situations (Katz & Kahn, 1978). Role ambiguity refers to unclear role information and unclear role expectations. In work situations with high role ambiguity, individuals do not know exactly what is expected from them and where to put their priorities while working. Individuals who experience role ambiguity report more negative affective reactions to their jobs (Jackson & Schuler, 1985). We assume that role ambiguity is negatively related to psychological detachment from work during off-job time. Individuals who lack information about their roles and the associated expectations cannot be completely sure about which tasks to accomplish and how to proceed. For example, in situations of high role ambiguity individuals do not get unequivocal answers to their (implicit) questions about which tasks to pursue. As a consequence, it is more likely that individuals will continue to ponder these questions during off-job time. In cases of low role ambiguity, however, individuals will know what to do and how to do it; there will be no need to be mentally preoccupied with one's job when away from the workplace.

Role conflict refers to conflicting role expectations. Individuals in a role conflict situation will face diverse or even contradictory expectations expressed by others in the environment (e.g., supervisors or co-workers). Role conflict was found to be associated with negative affective reactions to one's jobs (Jackson & Schuler, 1985). Being exposed to conflicting expectations from others is a stressful experience that may cause individuals to think about which expectation to satisfy—and which to disregard. Alternatively, individuals may reflect about how to reconcile the conflicting expectations. In any case, role conflict will make it more likely that an individual keeps thinking about his or her work. One can assume that individuals will continue to think about the conflicting expectations during their off-job time. Therefore, it will be difficult for them to psychologically detach from work when they are away from the workplace.

Hypothesis 1: Job stressors are negatively related to psychological detachment from work.

Job involvement

Job involvement is a specific belief about one's present job and refers to the degree to which one's job can satisfy one's needs (Kanungo, 1982). Individuals with high job involvement identify more with their jobs and regard their job as highly important for their lives. Compared to individuals with low job involvement, for highly job-involved individuals their job is more closely linked to their self-esteem (Lodahl & Kejner, 1965; Thoits, 1991). Job involvement has been found to be positively related to effort, various facets of job satisfaction, organizational commitment, and low turnover intention (Brown, 1996). However, job involvement may also have negative side effects. For example, individuals with high job involvement were found to react more negatively to job stressors (Frone, Russell, & Cooper, 1995).

At the *conceptual* level, job involvement has to be differentiated from psychological detachment. Job involvement refers to the relevance the job has for one's life. It is a relatively stable belief that links one's job to one's self-esteem. In contrast, psychological detachment refers to specific behaviours and cognitive activities in a given off-job situation, for example when being at home. With respect to the *empirical* relationship, we assume that job involvement is negatively related to psychological detachment from work during off-job time. As job involvement refers to an individual's identification with his or her job, high job involvement implies that one puts great emphasis on one's job and the job plays a core role in one's life—or as Janssen (2003) put it, "workers with greater job involvement have psychologically more at stake" (p. 351). This great importance of the job implies a substantial concern for job-related issues. This concern may not only be felt when at the workplace but also at home. As a consequence one will even think about one's job when at home. Therefore, it is less likely that individuals with high job involvement psychologically detach from their jobs during evening hours as compared to individuals with low job involvement.

Hypothesis 2: Job involvement is negatively related to psychological detachment from work.

Recovery-related self-efficacy

Eden (2001b) has argued that self-fulfilling prophecies may be highly relevant to recovery processes. The core assumption is that the expectations individuals hold about their recovery episodes (e.g., vacations, weekends, free evenings) influence the probability of the event they expect. For example, when an individual expects that his or her well-being will improve when spending a nice evening with friends it is more likely that this individual will have a pleasurable evening and will recover from work stress than when this individual expects that he or she will continue to feel strained.

We refer to an individual's expectation of being able to benefit from recovery time and recovery opportunities as *recovery-related self-efficacy* and assume that recovery-related self-efficacy is an important predictor of psychological detachment from work during off-job time. If one expects that one can adequately recover during off-job time then one is more likely to initiate activities that help to detach from work and to recover. Even if job-related thoughts come into mind, one will regard these thoughts as transient that can be "overcome" soon. Therefore, one is less likely to dwell on job-related thoughts. However, if one expects that one will not succeed in recovering during off-job time, one will be less likely to initiate helpful activities. In addition, one will interpret job-related thoughts as a sign that it is impossible to detach and recover. As a consequence, one will be more inclined to continue ruminating on job-related issues.

Hypothesis 3: Recovery-related self-efficacy is positively related to psychological detachment from work.

THE PRESENT STUDY

Previous research on recovery was largely based on self-report data. When interpreting findings from studies that use only self-report data, associations due to common method variance cannot be ruled out completely (Podsakoff, MacKenzie, Lee, & Podsakoff, 2003). To address this problem at least partially, we assessed psychological detachment not only by a self-report measure, but additionally collected family ratings of psychological detachment.

One might argue that psychological detachment from work may not only be predicted by job stressors, job involvement, or recovery-related self-efficacy but by other individual difference variables, too. One prime individual difference variable that might be related to psychological detachment from work during off-job time is action-state orientation (Kuhl, 1994b). Action-state orientation refers to an individual's ability to allocate attention to the present situation and the task at hand (action orientation). It is opposed to an individual's tendency to ruminate about past situations and failures (state orientation). Therefore, when examining the relationship between job stressors, job involvement, and recovery-related self-efficacy on the one hand, and psychological detachment on the other hand, we will control for action-state orientation.

In addition, individuals differ largely with respect to the number of hours they work. With respect to psychological detachment one can assume that the number of hours worked differ substantially. Compared to the amount of time available to full-time employees, the time budget of part-time employees offers more hours to be devoted to other activities than to one's job. As a consequence, part-time employees might find it easier to psychologically detach from work during off-job time. In addition, it has been found that job involvement differs between part- and full-time employees (Thorsteinson, 2003). To rule out that relationships between our predictor variables on the one hand and psychological detachment on the other hand are attributable to differences in work hours between full-time and part-time employees, we will control for contract working hours in our analyses.

Finally, demographic variables might also be related to psychological detachment from work. For example, younger individuals might find it more difficult to psychologically detach from work because they might lack successful coping strategies that help in dealing with work-related problems. Women and individuals with children might find it easier to detach because they are more involved in household and childcare activities (e.g., Sonnentag, 2001) which might offer a distraction from work-related thoughts. Therefore, we will also control for age, gender, and number of children in our analyses.

METHOD

Sample

We collected data in 14 schools in the northern part of Germany. To recruit teachers for participation, we first approached the heads of the schools and explained the overall goal of the study. Subsequently, survey packages were distributed to a total of 332 teachers. These packages included a letter, a self-report questionnaire, a questionnaire to be completed by a family member, and a return envelope. The letter described the purpose of the study, emphasized voluntariness, anonymity, and confidentiality of responses. In each school a return box was installed. Study participants were asked to deposit the completed questionnaires in a sealed envelope in these boxes.

One-hundred-and-fifty-seven survey packages were returned, with a response rate of 47.2%. Due to missing data in some of the self-report variables the total sample size was reduced to 148. Out of these 148 study participants, 121 individuals (81.8%) returned family reports of psychological detachment. The majority (85.1%) of these family reports were provided by the spouse, the remaining family reports came from grown-up children (6.6%) or other persons (5.0%); 3.3% did not report their type of relationship.

On average, study participants were 47.5 years old ($SD = 8.8$); 67% of the sample were female, 33% were male. The majority of the participants

(82.4%) were living with a partner, 12.8% were living alone. Some participants (4.7%) were living as single parents with their children or were living with another person neither being their partner nor their child. In total, 26.4% of the participants had no children, 14.9% had one child, 42.6% had two children, and 16.3% had three or more children.

Overall, study participants were highly experienced in their jobs with a mean teaching experience of 20.9 years $(SD = 10.6)$. Mean teaching hours per week were 21.4 hours $(SD = 5.6)$. On average, study participants reported that they worked 5.6 days $(SD = 0.90)$ per week for their job—although no one taught on Saturdays or Sundays. More specifically, 0.7% of the sample worked on three days, 8.1% worked on four days, 35.1% worked on five days, 37.2% worked on six days, and 18.9% worked on seven days.

We compared the subsample of teachers who provided family ratings of detachment with those who did not provide such a rating. There were no significant differences in gender, age, teaching experience, hours taught per week, or days worked for school per week. However, and not surprisingly, teachers who did not provide family ratings were more often living alone and had fewer children.

Measures

We used questionnaires to assess our data. Job stressors, job involvement, recovery-related self-efficacy, psychological detachment, and control variable measures were provided by the focal study participants. We assessed an additional detachment measure from one of the focal study participants' family members. All items were in German. Table 1 shows means, standard deviations, zero-order correlations, and Cronbach's αs for all study variables.

Job stressors. We assessed various aspects of job stressors: workload, role ambiguity, and role conflict. We measured workload with five 5-point Likert items from the time pressure scale developed by Semmer (1984) and Zapf (1993). This measure is frequently used in German-speaking countries for assessing quantitative workload (Frese, 1985; Garst, Frese, & Molenaar, 2000; Semmer, Zapf, & Greif, 1996). Sample items were "How often do you work under time pressure?" and "How often does it happen that you do not take a break or take a break late because of a high amount of work?" Cronbach's α was .83. We assessed role ambiguity with five 5-point Likert items from the measure developed by Semmer (1984) and Zapf (1993). A sample item was: "How often do you have to make decisions at your job without having sufficient information available?" Cronbach's α was .68. For measuring role conflict we used eight items from Rizzo, House, and Lirtzman's (1970) role conflict scale. A sample item was: "I receive incompatible requests from two or more people". Cronbach's α was .86.

TABLE 1
Means, standard deviations, zero-order correlations, and Cronbach's alpha for study variables

	M	SD	1	2	3	4	5	6	7	8	9	10	11	12
1. Gender	0.67	0.47	—											
2. Age	47.53	8.81	-.12	—										
3. Number of children	1.54	1.16	-.04	.39	—									
4. Action-state orientation	0.45	0.28	-.14	-.00	.01	.82								
5. Job involvement	4.30	0.94	.10	-.01	-.07	-.00	.86							
6. Recovery-related self-efficacy	3.60	1.38	-.16	.13	.19	.34	-.25	.90						
7. Teaching load	21.43	5.57	-.13	-.09	-.15	.02	-.18	-.08	—					
8. Workload	3.14	0.83	.07	-.14	-.22	-.16	.31	-.41	.10	.83				
9. Role ambiguity	1.98	0.61	-.09	-.17	-.23	-.06	.12	-.28	.10	.37	.68			
10. Role conflict	2.62	0.77	-.07	-.14	-.21	.01	.13	-.26	-.10	.41	.58	.86		
11. Self-reported detachment	2.81	0.83	-.11	.15	.23	.23	-.29	.62	-.13	-.46	-.21	-.21	.84	
12. Family-reported detachment	2.77	0.78	-.14	.08	.17	.14	-.29	.40	-.04	-.43	-.16	-.22	.44	.82

$N = 148$ (except for correlations with family-reported detachment). $N = 121$ for correlations with family-reported detachment. Correlations greater than .16 are significant with $p < .05$ (except for family-reported detachment). Correlations greater than .21 are significant with $p < .01$ (except for family-reported detachment).

Gender: 1 = male. 2 = female.

Job involvement.   We assessed job involvement with four items from the scale developed by Kanungo (1982) and adapted by Frone, Russell, and Cooper (1992). A sample item was: "I am very much personally involved with my job". Cronbach's α was .86.

Recovery-related self-efficacy.   To assess recovery-related self-efficacy we used a 6-item scale developed by Kodja (2003). These items refer to an individual's confidence to be able to recover from work even under adverse circumstances. The items were: "I feel confident to be able to recover during off-job time even when ... I am tired", "... when I feel depressed", "...when I am worrying", "...when I am angry about something", "... when I have a lot of things to do", and "... when something unexpected happens". Respondents were asked to answer these items on a 7-point Likert scale. Cronbach's α was .90.

Psychological detachment.   We measured self-reported psychological detachment with four items from the Recovery Questionnaire developed by Sonnentag and Fritz (2005). Items had to be answered on a 5-point Likert scale. Sample items were: "During evenings, I gain distance to my job requirements" and "During evenings, I don't think about work at all." Cronbach's α was .84.

One might argue that psychological detachment, recovery-related self-efficacy, and job involvement show substantial conceptual overlap. Therefore, we conducted an exploratory factor analysis with varimax rotation. This factor analysis resulted in a clear three-factor solution with Eigenvalues of the three factors greater than 1. All items loaded on their respective factors with factor loadings $\geq$ .60 and cross-loading not exceeding .42. Therefore, we are confident that psychological detachment, recovery-related self-efficacy, and job involvement are distinct concepts.

In addition to the self-report measure of psychological detachment we collected family-report measures of psychological detachment. More specifically, we asked our study participants to hand a one-page questionnaire to another person with whom the study participant had close contact on an every-day basis. We suggested that this other person should be someone like the spouse or partner, or a grown-up child living in the same household. This other person was asked to report whether the focal person detaches from work during leisure time. Specifically, the family member was asked to complete four 5-point Likert-type items that were identical to the self-report items (sample item: "During evenings he/she gains distance to his/her job requirements"). Cronbach's α was .82. The correlation between this family-reported detachment measure and self-reported detachment was $r = .44, p < .001$.

To examine whether psychological detachment matters with respect to recovery, we collected a more direct measure of recovery. Specifically, study participants had to answer four 5-point Likert items that assessed the subjective recovery experience (sample items: "During evenings I feel recovered mentally" and "During evenings I am full of new energy"). Cronbach's α of this scale was .87. We tested the factor structure of the (self-reported) psychological detachment and this recovery measure with an exploratory factor analysis with varimax rotation. This factor analysis resulted in a two-factor solution with all detachment items loading on one and all recovery items loading on the other factor. Next, we correlated the two detachment measures with the recovery measure. Zero-order correlations were $r = .62$ ($p < .001$) for self-reported detachment and $r = .26$ ($p < .01$) for family-reported detachment. This analysis shows that psychological detachment is positively related to the recovery experience.

Control variables.   As control variables we assessed age, gender, and number of children with single items. In addition, we assessed action-state orientation with the 12-item preoccupation subscale of the Action Control Scale (ACS-90) developed by Kuhl (1990, 1994a). A sample item was "If I've worked for four weeks on one project and then everything goes completely wrong: (a) It takes me a long time to adjust to it. (b) It bothers me for a while, but then I don't think about it any more." with (a) indicating a state-oriented answer and (b) indicating an action-oriented answer. Some items were recoded so that high scores represented high action orientation. Cronbach's α was .82. As an additional control variable we measured teaching load. Specifically, we assessed the number of hours spent on teaching with a single item directly asking: "How many hours do you teach in class per week?" This measure of teaching load differs from the workload measure. Teaching load refers to the contract hours of teaching but does not include the hours needed for other job-related activities such as preparing lessons. Workload refers to the subjective experience of having too much to do.

RESULTS

Test of hypotheses

We tested our hypotheses with a multiple regression approach in which we entered control variables (gender, age, number of children, action orientation, teaching load) in Step 1, and our core predictor variables (i.e., job involvement, recovery-related self-efficacy, workload, role ambiguity, and role conflict) in Step 2. For self-reported detachment results are displayed in Table 2; for family-reported detachment, results are displayed in Table 3.

TABLE 2
Results from multiple regression analysis predicting self-reported detachment

	Step 1		Step 2	
	Beta	t	Beta	t
Gender	− .069	− 0.855	.004	0.055
Age	.050	0.584	.025	0.364
Number of children	.199	2.333*	.077	1.096
Action-state orientation	.221	2.802**	.033	0.480
Teaching load	− .107	− 1.343	− .082	− 1.197
Job involvement			− .121	− 1.764[a]
Recovery-related self-efficacy			.489	6.518***
Workload			− .204	− 2.646**
Role ambiguity			.048	0.606
Role conflict			− .002	− 0.030
R^2		.13		.46
F		4.128**		11.953***
ΔR^2		.13		.34
F		4.128**		17.410***

*$p < .05$, **$p < .01$, ***$p < .001$. [a]$p = .080$.

TABLE 3
Results from multiple regression analysis predicting family-reported detachment

	Step 1		Step 2	
	Beta	t	Beta	t
Gender	− .119	− 1.244	− .121	− 1.395
Age	.010	0.104	− .036	− 0.410
Number of children	.148	1.526	.017	0.183
Action-state orientation	.119	1.297	− .011	− 0.124
Teaching load	− .045	− 0.480	− .044	− 0.504
Job involvement			− .174	− 2.029*
Recovery-related self-efficacy			.244	2.592*
Workload			− .279	− 2.859**
Role ambiguity			.070	0.695
Role conflict			− .093	− 0.904
R^2		.06		.30
F		1.489		4.595***
ΔR^2		.06		.23
F		1.489		7.293***

*$p < .05$, **$p < .01$, ***$p < .001$.

Table 2 shows that the control variables gender, age, number of children, action-state orientation, and teaching load accounted for 13% of the variance in self-reported detachment. Number of children and action-state orientation were significant predictors of psychological detachment. Job involvement, recovery-related self-efficacy, and the three job stressors entered in Step 2 contributed significantly to the prediction of self-reported detachment. Workload showed a significant negative relationship and recovery-related self-efficacy showed a significant positive relationship with self-reported detachment. The negative regression weight of job involvement was marginally significant. Role ambiguity and role conflict were no significant predictors of self-reported detachment.

With respect to family-reported detachment the control variables showed no significant relationships with psychological detachment (Table 3). The core predictor variables entered in Step 2 contributed to a significant increase in R^2. Job involvement, recovery-related self-efficacy, and workload were significant predictors of family-reported detachment with job involvement and workload showing a negative and recovery-related self-efficacy showing a positive regression weight.

Taken together, workload was a significant negative predictor of both self-reported and family-reported detachment. Neither role ambiguity nor role conflict was significantly related to psychological detachment. Thus, Hypothesis 1 received partial support. Job involvement was a negative predictor of both self-reported and family-reported detachment, lending support for Hypothesis 2. Recovery-related self-efficacy was significantly related to both self-reported and family-reported detachment indicating support for Hypothesis 3.

Additional analyses

One might assume that recovery-related self-efficacy and low job involvement are not only directly related to psychological detachment from work during off-job time. Recovery-related self-efficacy and job involvement may also moderate the relationship between job stressors and psychological detachment. More specifically, it can be argued that recovery-related self-efficacy attenuates the proposed negative relationship between job stressors and psychological detachment because individuals with high recovery-related self-efficacy may be successful in distancing themselves from work during off-job time, even when they have been confronted with job stressors. High job involvement may even strengthen the negative relationship between job stressors and psychological detachment. Individuals with a high degree of job involvement take their job very seriously and therefore job stressors might be more important for them than for individuals low on job involvement. Therefore, it will be more difficult for them to mentally "switch off" when facing job stressors.

In additional multiple regression analyses we tested for these inter-action effects. We computed interaction terms between recovery-related self-efficacy and the three job stressor variables (i.e., Recovery-related self-efficacy × Workload, Recovery-related self-efficacy × Role ambiguity, Recovery-related self-efficacy × Role conflict) and between job involvement and the three job stressor variables (i.e., Job involvement × Workload, Job involvement × Role ambiguity, Job involvement × Role conflict) and entered these interaction terms in an additional step in the regression equations. To minimize problems of multicollinearity, we entered the interaction terms with recovery-related self-efficacy and with job involvement in two distinct steps. Explained variance in self-reported detachment did not increase after entering interaction terms with recovery-related self-efficacy, $\Delta R^2 = .01$, $F = 0.500$, ns, nor after entering interaction terms with job involvement, $\Delta R^2 = .02$, $F = 2.003$, ns. Also variance explained in family-reported detachment did not improve after entering interaction terms with recovery-related self-efficacy, $\Delta R^2 = .03$, $F = 1.581$, ns, nor after entering interaction terms with job involvement, $\Delta R^2 = .03$, $F = 1.729$, ns. Therefore, one has to conclude that neither recovery-related self-efficacy nor job involvement moderate the relationship between job stressors and detachment.

DISCUSSION

This study addressed the relationship between job stressors, job involvement, recovery-related self-efficacy on the one hand and psychological detachment from work during evening hours on the other hand. Analyses showed a negative relationship between a high workload and psychological detachment. Moreover, individuals with high job involvement and low recovery-related self-efficacy were less likely to psychologically detach from work during off-job time. Job involvement and recovery-related self-efficacy did not moderate the relationship between job stressors and psychological detachment.

With respect to workload, this study confirms findings from earlier studies that revealed that quantitative workload and high strain jobs were related to low detachment during off-job time (Sonnentag & Bayer, 2005) and continued rumination about one's job during evening hours (Cropley & Millward Purvis, 2003). Interestingly, role ambiguity and role conflict were not significant predictors of psychological detachment. There are several reasons why workload rather than role ambiguity and role conflict is related to low detachment. First, workload scores were higher and therefore workload might be experienced as more stressful than role ambiguity and role conflict. Thus, workload might matter more for the teachers. As a consequence, they may continue thinking about their job during off job time. Second, it might be that teachers feel that they can deal with workload only by working longer hours or by working faster. Therefore, they may experience a permanent pressure to be mentally busy with their job—even during off-job time. The reduction of role conflict and role ambiguity, however, may be attributed to external sources such as school management and policy makers and therefore, the need to keep oneself occupied with job-related issues is lower. Third, it might be that all three types of role stressors (workload, role conflict, role ambiguity) might be associated with stressful job-related thoughts at home. However, it might be more likely that one is more likely to work long hours at home when facing workload than when facing role conflict or role ambiguity. Thus, it might be that the fact of working a great deal at home makes detachment difficult because work-related issues are very salient when at home. Fourth, when interpreting the findings it has to be taken into account that most teachers in our sample had long years of experience. Thus, average role ambiguity was particularly low, implying that teachers knew rather well what was expected from them. Therefore, it was unlikely that ambiguous role expectations kept study participants thinking about their job during off-job time.

Our study showed a negative relationship between job involvement and psychological detachment from work during off-job time. Individuals who are highly involved are less able or less willing to psychologically detach from work during off-job time. This finding adds to other research that pointed to a potential dark side of high job involvement. For example, studies have shown a stronger relationship between job stressors and poor psychological health in highly job-involved than in low job-involved individuals (Frone et al., 1995). In addition to the identity-based interpretation of this differential relationship offered in earlier research, our study suggests that low psychological detachment from work during off-job time might be the mediator underlying relationship between job involvement and impaired psychological health in highly job-involved individuals. Although our cross-sectional study does not warrant a causal interpretation of the relationship between job involvement and low psychological detachment, one may speculate that high job involvement might have some drawbacks in individuals' personal lives. In addition, it has to be noted that contingent on the specific sources of high job involvement the health-related consequences of job involvement may differ.

Recovery-related self-efficacy turned out to be a powerful predictor of psychological detachment. Individuals who are confident they can use their off-job time to recover, even under adverse conditions, report more psychological detachment from work during off-job time. This finding is in line with numerous research findings on the positive effects of task-related self-efficacy (Bandura, 1997) and supports the theoretical argument put forward by Eden (2001b).

Most of the findings were rather stable for the two detachment measures, namely self-reported and family-reported detachment. Therefore, we can be sure that the relationships found between workload, job involvement, and recovery-related self-efficacy on the one hand and psychological detachment on the other hand cannot be attributed to common method variance. By having included a family rating of psychological detachment in our analysis, we have overcome one of the shortcomings of many previous studies on recovery. However, it has to be noted that self-reported and family-reported detachment were only moderately related, suggesting that the focal person and his or her family member did not completely agree in their perception of psychological detachment. Nevertheless, the correlation between self-reported and family-reported detachment is within the usual range of correlations between self-report and peer-report measures (Harris & Schaubroeck, 1988; Mabe & West, 1982).

Additional analyses have shown that neither recovery-related self-efficacy nor job involvement moderated the relationship between job stressors and psychological detachment. This finding implies that workload is related to low self-reported and low family-reported detachment—irrespective of an individual's level of recovery-related self-efficacy or his or her job involvement.

Limitations and avenues for future research

This study is not without limitations. First, we used a cross-sectional study design. Therefore, we may not draw any conclusions about causality. For example, correlations between study variables might be attributable to third variables. Moreover, it might not only be that workload or job involvement lead to low psychological detachment but also that the experience of low psychological detachment might affect perceptions of workload and job involvement. With respect to the relationship between recovery-related self-efficacy and psychological detachment, it is plausible to assume reciprocal effects with recovery-related self-efficacy enhancing psychological detachment and with psychological detachment in turn affecting recovery-related self-efficacy. To rule out the explanation referring to third variables we controlled for a range of demographic and other variables. Nevertheless, we admit that with our cross-sectional design we cannot address all causality issues satisfactorily. Here, longitudinal or experimental studies are required.

Second, we conducted our study with participants from one single profession what might limit the generalizability of our findings. Teachers are a specific group as they regularly accomplish job-related tasks in their homes. Thus, they spend many hours at home and at the same time they use their home as part of their working environment. This situation might make psychological detachment particularly difficult—even after having finished work. However, although it is reasonable to assume relatively low mean detachment scores in teachers, it is less plausible to assume that the relationship patterns between our study variables differ between teachers and other occupational groups. Clearly, future research should study other professions and should examine whether findings generalize across different work settings.

Third, we assessed job-stressors with a self-report measure. Therefore, our study does not provide a clear answer to the question whether actual workload or perceived workload is related to low psychological detachment. Future studies should aim at additionally assessing job stressors with more objective measures (cf. Semmer, Grebner, & Elfering, 2004).

Our assumption is that psychological detachment from work is a positive experience and that it promotes psychological well-being. However, one might argue that staying "attached" to one's job during evening hours may also have a positive side and may not necessarily impede well-being (Fritz & Sonnentag, 2005). For example, after having encountered a pressing problem at school, it might be necessary to continue thinking about this problem and to develop ideas about how to solve it while at home. Coming up with an innovative solution might not only have a positive effect for the persons involved in the problem, it might also provide some relief for the person who is thinking about the problem and who does not detach. This might be particularly the case for individuals with high job involvement. Therefore, future research should examine under which conditions low psychological detachment has positive as opposed to negative effects. However, based on past research (Etzion et al., 1998; Sonnentag & Bayer, 2005) and the positive correlation between psychological detachment and subjective feelings of recovery found in the present study, we assume that negative correlates of low psychological detachment are more widespread than positive ones.

In this study, we focused on job stressors, job involvement, and recovery-related self-efficacy as predictors of psychological detachment. In addition, more family-related experiences might also be relevant for psychological detachment from work. Positive experiences at home such as having an enjoyable evening with one's partner or joyfully playing with one's children may help in psychologically detaching from work. Paradoxically, more negative off-job experiences may also foster psychological detachment from work. For example, having an argument with one's partner or conflicts with the children may distract from job-related thoughts and therefore may enhance psychological detachment—without having a recovering effect. Therefore, we suggest that future studies put more emphasis on the family situation as a potential predictor of psychological detachment and recovery. One may speculate that distraction might help in psychologically detaching from work but that psychological detachment only unfolds its recovery potential when associated with a positive rather than a stressful experience.

Practical implications

Our study offers some practical implications. Because the study does not provide an unequivocal answer to the question of causality, these conclusions should be regarded as preliminary. To improve psychological detachment from work during off-job time, it is crucial to address the issue of high workload. First, objective workload should be kept within moderate limits and time pressure should be reduced. These measures will allow teachers to spend less time on job-related tasks at home, which will probably foster psychological detachment. In addition, by reducing workload and time pressure, work will be experienced as less stressful, thus making it less likely that one has to think about job-related problems during off-job hours. Second, if objective workload and time pressure cannot be reduced substantially, it is important to teach time management skills so that individuals will be able to handle their workload more easily (Koch & Kleinmann, 2002; Peeters & Rutte, 2005). It can be expected that time management skills will help to finish work tasks more quickly what in turn will help in detaching from work during off-job time.

Moreover, to improve psychological detachment during off-job time it seems promising to increase recovery-related self-efficacy. We assume that— similar to factors that increase task-related self-efficacy (Bandura, 1997)— enactive mastery experience, vicarious experience, and verbal persuasion are important here. However, as long as an individual finds it difficult to psychologically detach from work and to recover during off-job time, it is not very likely that mastery experience and vicarious learning occur. Rather, these individuals may end up in a vicious cycle: Individuals with low recovery-related self-efficacy will expect that they cannot sufficiently recover during off-job time. As a consequence, psychological detachment from work when being at home will be low. Low detachment will make recovery unlikely and therefore, they will miss the opportunity to experience that they can recover. Recovery-related self-efficacy will remain low. To overcome this vicious cycle, trainings and counselling approaches that foster recovery-related self-efficacy might be necessary and beneficial.

Conclusion

Recovery from job stress is a complex phenomenon. In this study, we focused on psychological detachment from work during off-job time—an experience that has been shown to be important for recovery (Etzion et al., 1998; Sonnentag & Bayer, 2005). The study showed that psychological detachment is not an arbitrary event but closely related to individual and job-related factors. We hope that this study adds a little to our understanding of the recovery phenomenon and will stimulate further research in order to understand more fully how individuals can recover successfully from job stress.

REFERENCES

Bandura, A. (1997). *Self-efficacy: The exercise of control.* New York: Freeman.

Brown, S. P. (1996). A meta-analysis and review of organizational research on job involvement. *Psychological Bulletin, 120,* 235–255.

Cropley, M., & Millward Purvis, L. J. (2003). Job strain and rumination about work issues during leisure time: A diary study. *European Journal of Work and Organizational Psychology, 12,* 195–207.

De Lange, A. H., Taris, T. W., Kompier, M. A. J., Houtman, I. L. D., & Bongers, P. M. (2003). "The very best of the millennium": Longitudinal research and the demand–control–(support) model. *Journal of Occupational Health Psychology, 8,* 282–305.

Eden, D. (2001a). Job stress and respite relief: Overcoming high-tech tethers. In P. L. Perrewé & D. C. Ganster (Eds.), *Research in occupational stress and well-being: Exploring theoretical mechanisms and perspectives* (pp. 143–194). Amsterdam, The Netherlands: JAI Press.

Eden, D. (2001b). Vacations and other respites: Studying stress on and off the job. In C. L. Cooper & I. T. Robertson (Eds.), *International review of industrial and organizational psychology* (pp. 121–146). Chichester, UK: Wiley.

Etzion, D., Eden, D., & Lapidot, Y. (1998). Relief from job stressors and burnout: Reserve service as a respite. *Journal of Applied Psychology, 83,* 577–585.

Frese, M. (1985). Stress at work and psychosomatic complaints: A causal interpretation. *Journal of Applied Psychology, 70,* 314–328.

Fritz, C., & Sonnentag, S. (2005). Recovery, health, and job performance: Effects of weekend experiences. *Journal of Occupational Health Psychology, 10,* 187–199.

Frone, M. R., Russell, M., & Cooper, M. L. (1992). Antecedents and outcomes of work-to-family-conflict: Testing a model of work–family interface. *Journal of Applied Psychology, 82,* 65–78.

Frone, M. R., Russell, C. J., & Cooper, M. L. (1995). Job stressors, job involvement and employee health: A test of identity theory. *Journal of Occupational and Organizational Psychology, 68,* 1–11.

Garst, H., Frese, M., & Molenaar, P. C. M. (2000). The temporal factor of change in stressor–strain relationships: A growth curve model on a longitudinal study in East Germany. *Journal of Applied Psychology, 85,* 417–438.

Grebner, S., Semmer, N. K., & Elfering, A. (2005). Working conditions and three types of well-being: A longitudinal study with self-report and rating data. *Journal of Occupational Health Psychology, 10,* 31–43.

Harris, M. M., & Schaubroeck, J. (1988). A meta-analysis of self–supervisor, self–peer, and peer–supervisor ratings. *Personnel Psychology, 41,* 43–62.

Jackson, S. E., & Schuler, R. S. (1985). A meta-analysis and conceptual critique of research on role ambiguity and role conflict in work settings. *Organizational Behavior and Human Performance, 33,* 1–21.

Janssen, O. (2003). Innovative behavior and job involvement at the price of conflict and less satisfactory relations with co-workers. *Journal of Occupational and Organizational Psychology, 76,* 347–364.

Kahn, R. L., & Byosiere, P. (1992). Stress in organizations. In M. D. Dunnette & L. M. Hough (Eds.), *Handbook of industrial and organizational psychology* (2nd ed., Vol. 3, pp. 571–650). Palo Alto, CA: Consulting Psychologists Press.

Kanungo, R. N. (1982). Measurement of job and work involvement. *Journal of Applied Psychology, 67*, 341–349.

Katz, D., & Kahn, R. L. (1978). *The social psychology of organizations* (2nd ed.). New York: Wiley.

Koch, C. J., & Kleinmann, M. (2002). A stitch in time saves nine: Behavioural decision-making explanations for time management problems. *European Journal of Work and Organizational Psychology, 11*, 199–217.

Kodja, S. (2003). *Erholung von der Arbeit. Die Untersuchung von Selbstwirksamkeit und weiteren Moderatorvariablen.* Unpublished diploma thesis, Technical University of Braunschweig, Braunschweig, Germany.

Kuhl, J. (1990). *Der Fragebogen zur Erfassung von Handlungskontrolle nach Erfolg, Mißerfolg und prospektiv HAKAMP 90.* Osnabrück, Germany: University of Osnabrück.

Kuhl, J. (1994a). Action versus state orientation: Psychometric properties of the action control scale (ACS-90). In J. Kuhl & J. Beckmann (Eds.), *Volition and personality: Action versus state orientation* (pp. 47–59). Seattle, WA: Hogrefe & Huber.

Kuhl, J. (1994b). A theory of action and state orientations. In J. Kuhl & J. Beckmann (Eds.), *Volition and personality: Action versus state orientation* (pp. 9–46). Seattle, WA: Hogrefe & Huber.

Lodahl, T. M., & Kejner, M. (1965). The definition and measurement of job involvement. *Journal of Applied Psychology, 49*, 24–33.

Mabe, P. M., & West, S. G. (1982). Validity of self-evaluations of ability. *Journal of Applied Psychology, 67*, 180–196.

Peeters, M. A. G., & Rutte, C. G. (2005). Time management behavior as a moderator for the job demand–control interaction. *Journal of Occupational Health Psychology, 10*, 64–75.

Podsakoff, P. M., MacKenzie, S. B., Lee, J.-Y., & Podsakoff, N. P. (2003). Common method biases in behavioral research: A critical review of the literature and recommended remedies. *Journal of Applied Psychology, 88*, 879–903.

Rizzo, J. R., House, R. J., & Lirtzman, S. I. (1970). Role conflict and ambiguity in complex organizations. *Administrative Science Quarterly, 15*, 150–163.

Semmer, N. (1984). *Streßbezogene Tätigkeitsanalyse* [Stress-oriented analysis task-analysis]. Weinheim, Germany: Beltz.

Semmer, N. K., Grebner, S., & Elfering, A. (2004). Beyond self-report: Using observational, physiological, and situation-based measures in research on occupational stress. In P. L. Perrewé & D. C. Ganster (Eds.), *Research in occupational stress and well-being: Emotional and physiological processes and positive intervention strategies* (Vol. 3, pp. 205–263). Amsterdam, The Netherlands: Elsevier.

Semmer, N., Zapf, D., & Greif, S. (1996). "Shared job strain": A new approach for assessing the validity of job stress measurements. *Journal of Occupational and Organizational Psychology, 69*, 293–310.

Sluiter, J. K., Frings-Dresen, M. H. W., van der Beek, A. J., & Meijman, T. F. (2001). The relation between work-induced neuroendocrine reactivity and recovery, subjective need for recovery, and health status. *Journal of Psychosomatic Research, 50*, 29–37.

Sluiter, J. K., van der Beek, A. J., & Frings-Dresen, M. H. W. (1999). The influence of work characteristics on the need for recovery and experienced health: A study on coach drivers. *Ergonomics, 42*, 573–583.

Sonnentag, S. (2001). Work, recovery activities, and individual well-being: A diary study. *Journal of Occupational Health Psychology, 6*, 196–210.

Sonnentag, S. (2003). Recovery, work engagement, and proactive behavior: A new look at the interface between non-work and work. *Journal of Applied Psychology, 88*, 518–528.

Sonnentag, S., & Bayer, U.-V. (2005). Switching off mentally: Predictors and consequences of psychological detachment from work during off-job time. *Journal of Occupational Health Psychology, 10*, 393–414.

Sonnentag, S., & Frese, M. (2003). Stress in organizations. In W. C. Borman, D. R. Ilgen, & R. J. Klimoski (Eds.), *Comprehensive handbook of psychology: Vol. 12. Industrial and organizational psychology* (pp. 453–491). New York: Wiley.

Sonnentag, S., & Fritz, C. (2005). Recovery Questionnaire. University of Konstanz and Bowling Green State University. *Manuscript in preparation.*

Sonnentag, S., & Zijlstra, F. R. H. (in press). Work characteristics and off-job time activities as predictors of need for recovery, well-being and fatigue. *Journal of Applied Psychology.*

Strauss-Blasche, G., Ekmekcioglu, C., & Marktl, W. (2000). Does vacation enable recuperation? Changes in well-being associated with time away from work. *Occupational Medicine, 50,* 167–172.

Thoits, P. A. (1991). On merging identity theory and stress research. *Social Psychology Quarterly, 54,* 101–112.

Thorsteinson, T. J. (2003). Job attitudes of part-time versus full-time workers: A meta-analytic review. *Journal of Occupational and Organizational Psychology, 76,* 151–177.

Westman, M., & Eden, D. (1997). Effects of a respite from work on burnout: Vacation relief and fade-out. *Journal of Applied Psychology, 82,* 516–527.

Westman, M., & Etzion, D. (2001). The impact of vacation and job stress on burnout and absenteeism. *Psychology and Health, 16,* 595–606.

Zapf, D. (1993). Stress-oriented analysis of computerized office work. *The European Work and Organizational Psychologist, 3,* 85–100.

EUROPEAN JOURNAL OF WORK AND
ORGANIZATIONAL PSYCHOLOGY
2006, 15 (2), 218–240

The contribution of various types of activities to recovery

John W. Rook and Fred R. H. Zijlstra

Department of Psychology, University of Surrey, and Surrey Sleep Research Centre, Guildford, UK

Stress and fatigue caused by work require daily recovery periods to offset future deleterious consequences to mental and physical health. The aim, therefore, of the current study was to gain insight into recovery processes during a normal week. The main hypotheses were that more time spent on work and work-related activities will have a negative impact on recovery, while more time spent on specific leisure activities would have a beneficial impact on recovery. Using diaries, 46 respondents (average age of 35) provided daily measures of fatigue, sleep, and time spent on recovery activities over 7 days. Recovery activities included time spent on activities that were social, physical, and work-related. Results indicated that whilst low effort and social activities are nonbeneficial to recovery, physical activities significantly predict recovery (i.e., the former increase fatigue whilst the latter decrease fatigue). Sleep quality also emerges as a significant predictor of recovery. The weekend respite appears important to recovery; however, the effect seems already to wane on Sunday evening in anticipation of the Monday workload. The article provides insights into leisure activities and the experience of fatigue.

Work-related stress (i.e., that attributed to the work environment) is now a leading cause of sickness absence and lost productivity within UK organizations (DWP, 2002; Moncrieff & Pomerleau, 2000). Sickness absence (some of which is due to stress) costs British Industry £23 billion each year (CBI, 2001) and it is estimated that 4% of the European Union's Gross National

Correspondence should be addressed to Professor Fred R. H. Zijlstra, Faculty of Psychology, Maastricht University, P.O. Box 616, NL 6200 MD Maastricht, The Netherlands. E-mail: fred.zijlstra@psychology.unimaas.nl

The authors would like to thank Dr A. Martin and the Occupational Health Team for helping to secure access to respondents. Gratitude is also extended to all those anonymous respondents who diligently kept diaries for a week, despite no obvious reward for their efforts. Furthermore we would like to thank the anonymous referees for their valuable comments and suggestions.

http://www.psypress.com/ejwop   DOI: 10.1080/13594320500513962

Product is spent on work-related mental health (O'Driscoll & Cooper, 2002). The prevalence of organizational stress and absenteeism, together with increasing work demands (Landsbergis, 2003), means that knowledge regarding the factors associated with insufficient recovery outside of work is important. This article attempts to address the topic of recovery activities after work during a normal working week in as far as they help to reduce the experience of fatigue and impact upon variables such as sleep, thus perhaps indicating the sorts of recovery patterns that are useful to maintain well-being.

The very nature of work requires investing resources and regulating the amount of effort expended in order to complete tasks effectively; inevitably this leads to fatigue as a result of these regulatory processes, both psychological and physiological. Current indications are that fatigue is a common complaint in the working population, with estimated prevalence rates between 22% and 38% in the Netherlands and UK respectively (Bültmann, Kant, Kasl, Beurskens, & van den Brandt, 2002a; Pawlikowska et al., 1994). Occupationally induced fatigue is the short-term effect of a working day and is primarily experienced *after* a day of work (Sluiter, 1999; Sluiter, Frings-Dresen, van der Beek, & Meijman, 2001). Self-reports of fatigue in bus drivers were related to increasing job demand, sleep complaints, and other psychosomatic maladies (Kompier, 1988). Rydstedt, Johansson, and Evans (1998) linked aspects of work stress to mental exhaustion after work and research by Sluiter, van der Beek, and Frings-Dresen (1999) showed that aspects of demand at work significantly contribute to a subjective need for recovery.

Sonnentag (2003) has also recently highlighted the importance of recovery for subsequent work behaviour to the extent that recovery during leisure influences both the degree of work engagement and proactive behaviour at work; daily fluctuations in behaviour and attitudes at work were also found to be related to opportunities to recover in the nonwork domain.

Meijman and Mulder's (1998) Effort-Recovery model provides a useful framework for the psychological study of workload (see Figure 1). Work demands (e.g., working hours) without sufficient recovery, can lead to negative load effects (e.g., fatigue) and longer term losses of function, physical and mental impairment. The work procedure results in physiological and psychological reactions, which in principle are reversible. Under normal conditions, psychobiological systems stabilize at baseline levels when stressors are absent—this return to prestressor levels of functioning is known as recovery, during which homeostasis of physiological and psychological systems is achieved (Craig & Cooper, 1992).

CYCLES OF WORK AND REST

It is intuitive that after work a period of recovery is required, perhaps achieved through simple rest or a change of activity. Fatigue and recovery

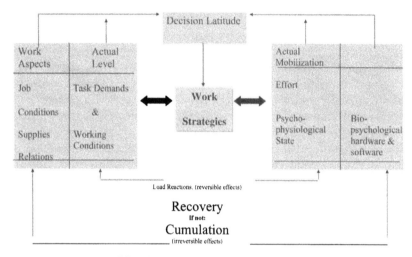

Figure 1.   Effort-Recovery Model (Meijman & Mulder, 1998).

are related concepts: Fatigue is the state that results from having been exposed to work demands, and recovery is the process of replenishing the depleted resources or rebalancing suboptimal systems. Occupationally induced fatigue is a central concept since failure to recover from its effects, evidenced in self-report data (e.g., Sluiter et al., 1999), can lead to negative consequences for health and organizational well-being. Indeed, elevated fatigue scores are used to identify those at risk of absenteeism or work disability (Bültmann et al., 2000), and could theoretically be used to identify individuals who have failed to recover from the short-term effects of a workday. Lack of recovery results in fatigue, thus fatigue can be used as a proxy to recovery; the term "recovery" is used in the remainder of the article to indicate a level of functioning or well-being, as indicated by reduction in fatigue scores.

Nonwork time is essential for recovery since (traditionally at least) work demands are absent. Whilst short-term load reactions are in principle reversible, time is a crucial variable. Occupationally induced fatigue is theorized not to be a problem if adequate recovery time is offered between two periods of exposure to work demands (Sluiter et al., 2001). If the psychological systems used during work are activated during recovery time, or the recovery is insufficient, a cumulative process involving prolonged fatigue, sleep complaints, and psychosomatic complaints may ensue.

Insufficient recovery is predicted to lead to a vicious cycle whereby extra effort needs to be invested at every successive work period in order to rebalance suboptimal psychophysiological states and to maintain perfor-mance (Sluiter et al., 1999; Sluiter et al., 2001). In the event of this "nonoptimal" state, occupationally induced fatigue may eventually develop into Chronic Fatigue Syndrome (CFS). Inadequate work-rest ratios are perhaps a causal factor in the development of CFS (Ray, Weir, Cullen, & Phillips, 1992). Sluiter et al. (2001) reported that higher levels of neuroendocrine reactivity after work (indicating poor recovery) predicted a higher number of reported health complaints. In a sense, lack of recovery is a type of sustained arousal. Burnout, which is associated with fatigue and inadequate coping (i.e., recovery), is another longer term health outcome that may be expected.

RESPITES AND RECOVERY PROCESSES

Research has demonstrated the beneficial and salutary effects of a temporary detachment and relief from job stressors on psychological and physiological variables (e.g., burnout, cortisol levels). Hobfoll and Shirom (2001) indicated that a relaxation period between stress episodes allows regrouping of resources. Westman and Eden's (1997) quasiexperimental studies revealed that burnout scores were lower during and after a 2-week vacation, although the relief was short-lived. Subsequent research has repeatedly demonstrated that stress levels fall during holiday periods (Eden, 2001). Etzion, Eden, and Lapidot (1998) extended the scope of this research to suggest that nonwork time of any sort helps to manage stress and relieve the symptoms of burnout; during and after vacation periods, sabbaticals, and leisure time generally, stress levels decrease and psychological symptoms such as burnout decrease, whilst well-being is enhanced. Physiological field studies have also evidenced decreased cortisol levels during leisure time, in addition to an increase in physiological reactions when work demands increase (e.g., Evans & Steptoe, 2001; Frankenhaeuser, 1989).

Although workers in Europe can normally expect a vacation of some sort during an average year, it seems that individuals require additional chances for recovery, especially when considering that the salutary effects of vacations have been found to fade out quickly, with dependant variables such as burnout and well-being rapidly returning to their prevacation levels soon after returning to work (Westman & Eden, 1997; Westman & Etzion, 2001). Thus, the daily recovery that occurs in the evenings after normal working days or during the traditional weekend respite becomes important to maintaining well-being and performance (Sonnentag, 2003). Various developments in the organization of work are believed to affect the time available for recovery; changes in work arrangements, i.e., the use of ICT, dual career families, homeworking, telecommuting, flexitime, sharing, and negotiating family responsibilities all affect the time available for recovery (Frankenhaeuser, Lundberg, Fredrikson, Melin, Tuomisto, Myrsten, et al., 1989; Roe et al., 1994; Zijlstra, Schalk, & Roe, 1996).

Based on these considerations and other indications that working hours and travel (daily commute to work) can increase stress and fatigue (Frankenhaeuser, 1989; Spurgeon & Cooper, 2001) our first hypothesis is:

Hypothesis 1: The amount of time spent on work and travel time will be negatively related to recovery. As stated before, reduction of fatigue will be used as a proxy of the recovery process. This means that we expect a positive association between the amount of time spent on work and travel and fatigue scores.

Emerging research has elucidated aspects of daily recovery by examining the contribution of leisure activities to recovery (Sonnentag, 2001). Using theoretical models to make predictions, such as the beneficial effects of low-effort and cognitively undemanding tasks following the Effort-Recovery model, Sonnentag's study examined the effects on recovery using the diary method. This research has been pivotal in providing the conceptual, theoretical, and empirical basis for the study of daily recovery activities. *Job-related activities*, such as preparing for work the next day, were predicted to inhibit recovery since recovery can only occur when work demands are absent. Similarly, *household activities* (e.g., cleaning) were predicted to prevent recovery since they often have a high degree of obligation and will threaten resources if performed whilst fatigued. *Low-effort activities* (e.g., watching TV) enable recovery since they are passive and place few demands on mental resources. *Social activities* (e.g., visiting friends) facilitate recovery since stressors are absent, thus facilitating return of prestressor levels of functioning. *Physical activities* are beneficial for recovery since different resources are used to those typically used at work. Moreover, physical activity has been extolled as a beneficial activity in its own right, becoming an "antidote" to anxiety and stress (Hull, 1990; Iso-Ahola, 1997; Iwasaki, 2001). Results from a recent longitudinal analysis confirms a strong inverse association between physical activity and the onset of chronic fatigue; those who exercise less than once a week are significantly more likely to be fatigued at follow-up (Bültmann, Kant, Kasl, Schroer et al., 2002). Sonnentag found that the amount of time spent on low-effort, physical, and social activities is conducive to recovery on a daily basis as measured by situational well-being (an affective component of the stress response), whilst job-related activities during nonwork time had deleterious effects. On the basis of these findings and to the extent that fatigue indicates the level of recovery and situational functioning we hypothesized that:

Hypothesis 2: The amount of time spent on household activities will be negatively related to recovery, as indicated by higher fatigue scores.

Hypothesis 3: The amount of time spent on low-effort, physical, and social activities will be positively to recovery, as indicated by a reduction in fatigue scores.

Studies of daily recovery have neglected to include measures of sleep, arguably a crucial recovery activity in its own right. Sleep is bound with fatigue and appears in scales designed to assess the impact of fatigue on daily functioning (Craig & Cooper, 1992; Ray et al., 1992). To the extent that sleep serves restorative functions and maintains performance (Campbell, 1992; Horne, 2001; Jouvet, 1999; Tilley & Brown, 1992), it is necessary to account for this phenomenon. Mikulincer, Babkoff, Caspy, and Sing (1989) report that sleep deprivation leads to fatigue, in turn reducing motivation. Research by Zijlstra and de Vries (2000) has indicated that sleep is important for recovery. Individuals with high levels of fatigue typically have fewer hours of sleep and require extra effort investment during the morning and afternoon in comparison to individuals with low levels of fatigue. Åkerstedt et al. (2002) report that aspects of job stress, failing to exercise, and doing household chores after work are all risk factors for disturbed sleep. In their model, high work demands lead to a difficulty unwinding and recovering after work; in turn this leads to sleep problems that consequently lead to higher demands the following day, i.e., needing to invest extra effort to maintain performance. It is reasonable to suppose that fatigue resulting from work stress and poor sleep quality will disincline individuals to engage in leisure activities. Moreover, levels of fatigue are suggested to be differentially effected by degree of sleep quality, rather than just quantity (e.g., Craig & Cooper, 1992). It has also been reported that the subjective component of sleep, as measured by self-report ratings of sleep quality, are more important than sleep quantity (Pilcher, 2000). To the extent that sleep quality may be more important than simply sleep quantity, it is reasonable to predict:

Hypothesis 4: Higher sleep quality will be positively related to recovery, as indicated by the proxy of fatigue scores.

Normally, people spend less time at work or work-related activities during the weekend. Therefore we expect that there will be an opportunity for recovery during the weekend. So, levels of fatigue should drop significantly over the weekend, and sleep quality should increase. Therefore our fifth hypothesis is:

Hypothesis 5: Fatigue scores will be higher during the week than during the weekend.

The present study aimed to gain some insight into the recovery processes during a normal working week and the extent to which the various leisure (nonwork) activities engaged in contribute to fatigue and thus recovery. The level of demand and effort of prototypical activities will also be highlighted. The present study also aimed to shed empirical light upon the work – rest cycle during a normal week whilst remaining nonintrusive. Daily recovery activities are investigated using a diary technique during which frequent, prestructured entries are made into paper diaries. Daily diary studies are ideal for tracking psychological phenomena over time (Harris, Daniels, & Briner, 2003) and capture data closer to the actual changes in fatigue levels, therefore making the data more reliable and less likely to suffer recall effects associated with retrospective measurements.

METHOD

Design

Diaries obtained data over 7 days, typical of a normal working week and weekend respite. Respondents logged the amount of time spent engaged in specific activities during nonwork time, whilst recording sleep patterns and completing a daily fatigue questionnaire. Diaries were similar to those previously used (cf. Sonnentag, 2000), but are unique in terms of measures, layout, and duration. Attention was given to the structure of diaries to ensure a user-friendly format, i.e., A5-sized flipchart format, with clear and precise examples of how to complete it. Respondents started filling out the diaries on the Sunday, running through to the following Sunday to obtain a full week's scores.

Participants

A sample of the working age population was recruited from three different organizations: 39% from a petroleum company, 46% from an IT company, and 15% from an opportunity sample. An Occupational Health fair provided a recruitment opportunity whereby appreciation of a "diary" could be supplemented by verbal instruction. Additional to verbal instruction during recruitment (to obtain informed consent and assurances of anonymity), clear and comprehensive instructions were given along with the diaries. Initially 109 individuals were approached for participation; a 42% response rate put the final sample at $N = 46$. With 18 men (39%) and 28 women (61%), mean age of respondents was 34.93 years (range $= 40$, $SD = 11$). Occupational roles varied: $n = 13$ respondents in technical and information technology roles, 10 managers, 10 administrators, 5 academics, 4 customer services and support workers, 2 directors, and 2 health professionals. The majority of respondents were single or living with a partner (59% single; 41% married); 59% had no children, 6.5% had one child, 24% had two children, 9% had three children, and 2% had four children ($M = 0.89$). There were no significant differences between the average weekly hours worked by males and females in the current sample in comparison to national averages (Office for National Statistics, 1998): males, $t(17) = -0.88$, $p > .05$ (two-tailed); females, $t(27) = -1.87$, $p > .05$ (two-tailed).

Measures

After-work activities. Respondents were provided with a table for each day containing a list of five prototypical activities;[1] these include: work-related tasks (e.g., responding to work e-mail), household tasks (e.g., cooking, cleaning, looking after children), low-effort tasks that are not demanding (e.g., listening to music), physical activities (e.g., playing sport), and social activities (e.g., visiting friends). Respondents logged the amount of time spent on each activity category per day (minutes and hours).

Fatigue. A measure of fatigue was used as a proxy of recovery, fatigue was assessed daily using the Checklist Individual Strength (CIS-20R; Vercoulen et al., 1994),[2] a 20-item self-report instrument measuring several aspects of fatigue rated on a 7-point scale (1 = "Yes, that is true", 7 = "No, that is not true"): the subjective feeling of fatigue (8 items, $\alpha = .86$), concentration (5 items, $\alpha = .92$), motivation (4 items, $\alpha = .76$), and physical activity (3 items, $\alpha = .80$). Subscales were scored to produce a composite ranging from 20 to 140 (total CIS $\alpha = .83$), higher scores indicating a greater level of fatigue, more concentration problems, reduced motivation, and less activity. Although epidemiological studies utilize predefined cut-off points to define fatigued cases, fatigue is best studied along a continuum (Bültmann, 2002); therefore higher scores are conceptualized as a lesser degree of recovery and vice versa. Respondents completed the CIS 30 minutes before retiring to allow for the ameliorating or inhibitive effects of intervening activity. The CIS questions individuals about fatigue during the past 2 weeks, but the instruction was changed by the authors for use in the present study to ask individuals to indicate how they felt during the current day. In this sense it was adapted to be a situational measure of fatigue. Items in the checklist remained the same. Internal consistency coefficients[3] indicated reliability of the measure.

---

[1] These prototypical activities are based on those previously used with minor additions (cf. Sonnentag, 2001).

[2] Copy obtained for use in the present research from the authors: J. H. M. M Vercoulen and G. Bleijenberg, University Hospital, Nijmegen.

[3] Cronbach's alpha levels are for CIS scores on Wednesday, giving an indication of how consistently fatigue levels are reported. Note: Alpha levels are similar to those previously reported, e.g., $\alpha = .9$ in Beurskens et al. (2000).

Sleep and sleep quality. Respondents kept a sleep diary (adapted from Morin, 1993) answering eight questions in the morning before leaving for work. This diary provided the following relevant parameters: total sleep time (TST), calculated from sleep onset latencies, and time in bed (TIB). A sleep efficiency index (SEI; %) is calculated from a ratio of TST and TIB. Two items allow respondents to rate sleep quality (SQ) and feeling upon arising (FUA): "When I got up this morning I felt" 1 = "Exhausted, 5 = "Very refreshed", and "Overall, my sleep last night was" 1 = "Very restless", 5 = "Very sound" ($\alpha = .86$). Previous empirical research validated the use of subjective measures of sleep and sleep quality (e.g., Killen, George, Marchini, Silverman, & Thoresen, 1982), which often correlate well with objective measures (i.e., Johns & Dore, 1978).

Work situation/demand variables. Respondents reported the amount of time spent (hours and minutes) on contractual work and travelling to and from work. Job characteristics were assessed using a 10-item questionnaire derived from Karasek's (1979) model (adapted by Cropley, Steptoe, & Joekes, 1999): Three dimensions were assessed: perceived demand (3 items), job control (3 items), and skill utilization (4 items), rated on a 4-point scale where 1 = "Strongly disagree", 4 = "Strongly agree".

Data analysis

Data were analysed using SPSS 11.0. Continuous time data was calculated for each respondent at both the day level and averaged across the total working week; thus for the proxy of fatigue, individual scores existed for each day of the week in addition to a summed and averaged total for the entire working week. Data were examined both at the week (averaging scores over the 7 days) and day level using *t*-tests and repeated measures ANOVA; pairwise comparisons were used to examine the significant differences in the major study variable scores for each day of the week. Zero-order correlations and regression analysis also enabled trends to be elucidated in addition to the predictor effects of work variables, recovery activities themselves, and also sleep variables. Although a cases-to-IV ratio of $N \geq 50 + 8m$ is suggested to run multiple regressions (Tabachnick & Fidell, 2001), the current sample size ($N = 46$) is adequate following a minimum requirement of five times more cases than IVs (Coakes & Steed, 2001). In addition to screening and replacement of missing values using mean substitution for a small amount of cases, no univariate outliers ($z > 3.29$) were identified. Distribution of continuous variables, such as time data and fatigue, was found to be normal with no significant skewness or kurtosis.

RESULTS

Relationship between after-work activities and recovery

Table 1 shows the zero-order correlations between the major study variables. Partial support for Hypothesis 3 was found: Time spent on physical activity is strongly negatively related to fatigue. However, low-effort and social activities (ns) were associated with increases in fatigue (i.e., recovery inhibitive). In support of Hypothesis 4, sleep is negatively related to fatigue, with sleep quality rather than quantity emerging as a significant variable.

To examine the specific contribution of leisure activities and the other main study variables to the experience of fatigue, a linear multiple regression was employed using fatigue as the dependent variable. However, first a regression analysis was run to ascertain whether demographic information significantly predicts elevated fatigue. In comparison to the constant-only model, the model with demographic information was not statistically significant ($F = 0.83$, $p = .53$), indicating that age, sex, marital status, presence of children, and occupation, as a set, do not reliably distinguish between fatigued individuals. With regards to individual predictors, beta statistics confirmed that none of the demographics reliably predicted fatigued status.

In the linear regression analysis all predictors were entered into one model simultaneously to ascertain their specific contribution to the increase or decrease in fatigue scores. No multivariate outliers (> 26.12) were identified using Mahalanobis distance, $p < .001$ criterion. Table 2 summarizes the results of the analysis. The model contained work hours and travel, recovery activities, and sleep parameters. As a set, these predictors were significant, $F(9, 36) = 5.47$, $p < .01$, accounting for 47% of the variance in fatigue levels.

Individual coefficients showed that work and travel time did not significantly contribute to fatigue (i.e., Hypothesis 1 was not supported). Time spent on household activities was not related to fatigue, i.e., Hypothesis 2 was not supported). Time spent on physical activities is significantly associated with decreases in the experience of fatigue, $\beta = -.39$, $t = -2.88$, $p < .01$. Individually, physical activity accounts for 9.67% of the variance in fatigue ($sr^2 - .276$) (partly support for Hypothesis 3). Sleep quality and feeling upon arising emerged as significant predictors, associated with decreases in fatigue as subjective ratings increase, $\beta = -.38$, $t = -2.55$, $p < .05$, accounting for 7.62% ($sr^2 - .311$) of the unique variance in fatigue scores (supporting Hypothesis 4). None of the other major study variables entered into the equation significantly predicted fatigue.

Cycle of recovery during the week

Figure 2 demonstrates the typical pattern of recovery over the course of a working week. Levels of fatigue are highest at the beginning of the week

TABLE 1

Zero-Order correlations between the major study variables ($N = 46$)

	M	SD	1	2	3	4	5	6	7	8	9	10	11	12	13
1. Fatigue‡	479.52	113.71	—												
2. Work-related[a]	203.3 (3.4)	352.9	-.05	—											
3. Household[a]	437.61 (7.3)	312.37	.05	-.04	—										
4. Low-effort[a]	885 (14.8)	514.81	.32*	-.14	.12	—									
5. Physical[a]	335.33 (5.6)	284.37	-.56**	.14	-.21	-.11	—								
6. Social[a]	824.78 (13.8)	380.9	.19	.13	-.16	.21	.13	—							
7. Work hrs	2445 (40.75)	418.7	-.13	.03	.04	.27*	.17	-.1	—						
8. Travel	209.54 (3.5)	132.4	.11	.12	-.11	-.21	-.05	-.1	.15	—					
9. Job strain	12.84	2.57	-.37**	.14	-.18	-.28*	.07	-.18	.25	.11	—				
10. TST[b]	2978 (49.6)	255.4	-.08	-.04	.01	.03	-.00	-.16	-.22	-.01	.07	—			
11. SEI[c]	87.25	5.06	-.35**	.11	.02	-.09	-.09	-.1	-.1	.15	.19	.53**	—		
12. SQ[d]	24.80	5.27	-.62**	-.11	-.15	-.16	.35**	-.09	.04	-.07	.28*	.26*	.44**	—	
13. FUA[e]	21.08	5.27	-.49**	-.09	-.23	-.22	.44**	-.27*	.23	.13	.31*	.24	.31*	.60**	—

‡Composite Fatigue score – summed CIS score over 7 days.

[a]Means and Standard Deviations for time spent on activities over the 7 day period in mins (hrs in parentheses).

[b]Total Sleep Time.

[c]Average Sleep Efficiency over 7 days.

[d,e]Composite Sleep Quality and Feeling upon arising [sum over 7 days] treated as continuous variable – Higher scores indicate better ratings of sleep quality and a more refreshed feeling when arising.

*$p < .05$; **$p < .01$ (one-tailed), Power = .9.

TABLE 2
Multiple Regression Analysis for variables predicting overall Fatigue scores ($N = 46$)

	Variable	β	t	Adjusted R^2
Model 1	Total time – Work-Related	−.012	−0.106	
	Total time – Household	−.100	−0.799	
	Total time – Low-Effort	.157	1.351	
	Total time – Physical	−.385**	−2.875	
	Total time – Social	.137	1.128	
	Sleep Quality + FUA	−.380*	−2.546	
	Average Overall Sleep Efficiency	−.191	−1.367	
	Time for Sleep	.149	1.087	
	Work + Travel Time	.017	0.130	
				$R^2 = .58$
				Adjusted $R^2 = .47$
				$R = .76$

$*p < .05; **p < .01.$

(Monday and Tuesday) with a sharp decline towards the end of the week and over the weekend—indeed both the linear and quadratic trend evidenced in Figure 2 is significant: linear $F(1, 45) = 12.81$, $p = .001$, $MS_{fatigue} = 4260$; quadratic $F(1, 45) = 9.33$, $p = .004$, $MS_{fatigue} = 1623$. To test the significance of these differences in fatigue over the week, pairwise comparisons revealed that there are significantly lower levels of fatigue on Sunday in comparison to all the other six days of the week (mean difference $= 12.50$, $p < .01$). Fatigue levels on Wednesday are significantly higher in comparison to both days during the weekend (mean difference $= 7.18$ and 13.47, respectively, $p < .05$). These results seem to be demonstrating the traditional function of a weekend "respite"; additional support is found from paired-samples t-tests: Fatigue during the week is significantly higher than fatigue over the weekend: Wed:Sat, $t(45) = 2.02$, $p = .04$, one-tailed; Wed:Sun, $t(45) = 4.22$, $p < .01$, one-tailed. This supports our fifth hypothesis. Correlations also suggest that higher fatigue during the weekend is associated with increased fatigue during the week: Wed – Sun, $r = .51$, $p \leq .01$, one-tailed; Mon – Sun, $r = .66$, $p \leq .01$, one-tailed. This suggests that lack of recovery during the weekend spills over into the working week (i.e., higher level of fatigue on Monday).

Interestingly, following previous research (e.g., Bültmann, 2002), 39% of participants in the present study would be considered at risk of sickness absence due to fatigue. This is utilizing a cut-off point of CIS20R > 76 whereby those individuals scoring above that score are at risk.

Effects of sleep on recovery

On average, respondents obtained just over 7 hours sleep per night with an average sleep efficiency of 87%. Sleep time increases over the weekend, as

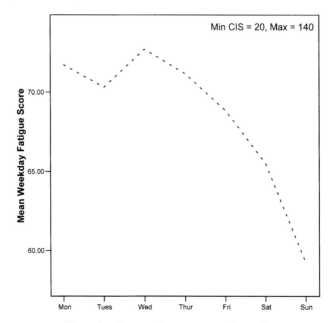

Figure 2.   Pattern of recovery over the week.

does the level of sleep quality and feelings upon arising. Correlations in Table 1 suggest that sleep is beneficial to recovery. Figure 3 shows the changes to the levels of sleep quality over the course of the week; highest levels observed over the weekend, with the lowest ratings typically observed on Monday morning. Pairwise comparisons from the repeated measures ANOVA showed that sleep quality ratings were significantly lower on Mondays, Tuesdays, and Thursdays in comparison to the Saturday sleep quality ratings (mean difference $= -0.46$, -0.45, and -0.44 respectively, $p < .05$). These results support the trend of a weekend respite in the sleep data. The pairwise comparisons also revealed a significant linear trend towards feeling more refreshed upon arising at the weekends: linear $F(1, 45) = 4.26$, $p = .045$, $MS_{fatigue} = 4.14$. Respondents reported significantly higher feelings upon arising (FUA) ratings on Saturday in comparison to all other working days (Mon–Fri mean difference $= 0.58$, $p < .05$). As can be seen in Figure 3, the lowest sleep quality ratings appear on Monday. However, it should be noted that these ratings are obtained on Monday morning, and refer to the Sunday's sleep episode. This may seem counterintuitive, but could indicate the anticipation of work demands.

Work variables

No significant effects or differences were found for travel time (Mon–Fri). Respondents report an average job strain of 12.84 ($SD = 2.57$). With 17.4%

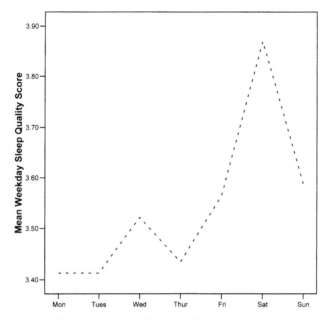

Figure 3. Pattern of sleep quality over the week.

($n = 8$) of the sample scoring 10 or below (good balance between demand/ control and low strain), 82.6% ($n = 38$) report higher strain in relation to their work. In comparison to previous studies;[4] however, the sample report significantly lower job strain scores, $t(45) = -7.8$, $p < .01$, two-tailed; thus respondents are not in a statistical sense "high strain".

DISCUSSION

The 46 respondents in the current study provided a wide range of data on the nature of recovery activities in relation to fatigue, sleep, and work situation variables. The results indicated that the amount of time spent on work and travel, and also the amount of time spent on work-related activities after work time did not contribute to predicting fatigue. Such a finding is consistent with some other studies who failed to find a direct association between number of hours worked and fatigue, in particular when people have a choice in deciding to work long hours (i.e., the higher level or white collar jobs, as in this sample; see Josten, 2002). People who spend a lot of time on their job usually do like their work, and thus do not experience fatigue. Contrary to prediction and recent findings (e.g., Sonnentag, 2001), low-effort and social activities were not conducive to recovery after work. Low-effort activities were even associated

---

[4]One-sample t-test with the mean statistic of 15.8 utilized by Cropley et al. (1999) to define those in high strain occupations.

with increases in fatigue. These activities are generally rather passive, and might not help to disengage from work activities. Their passive nature may even enhance feelings of fatigue and apathy and lethargy (Iso-Ahola, 1997). In this respect it should be brought to attention that our measure of fatigue was primarily a measure for the *subjective experience* of fatigue, rather than feelings of physical fatigue (after physical exercise), and therefore is believed to encompass a strong motivational component (Meijman, 1991; Zijlstra, 1993). Low-effort activities may therefore be beneficial for recovery from physical fatigue rather than from psychological fatigue. Moreover, since the diaries were unable to measure cognitive and psychological demands from work in a more detailed way (i.e., more than simple job strain questionnaire), it is impossible to conclude whether this result is due to low demands at work, thus causing low-effort activity during leisure to diminish recovery effects, or whether low-effort activities simply don't aid recovery. On the other hand it might be that people who feel fatigued may find themselves too tired to engage in any activities other than low-effort, thus suggesting that low-effort activities are not conducive to recovery. However, our study is consistent with findings that life-styles with low amounts of exercise results in more feelings of fatigue (e.g., Bültmann, Kant, Kasl, Schroer, Swaen, & Van den Brandt, 2002b; Jette, 1997).

The finding that the second hypothesis was not supported can also be explained from this perspective: Household activities, in particular caring for children, require active involvement. For that reason these activities help to disengage from the daily strains of work. Therefore they may even be seen as beneficial for recovery.

With regard to recovery conducive activities, it was demonstrated that greater time spent engaged in physical activity increased recovery levels, thus providing partial support for the second hypothesis; moreover, individuals with low levels of fatigue spent significantly more time engaged in physical activities. Although it was beyond the scope of the present research to isolate the precise mechanisms involved, such as the positive effects of endorphins (Steinberg et al., 1998), social support (Jones & Bright, 2001), and general well-being (Iwasaki, 2001), physical activity emerged as a strong individual factor benefiting recovery (with a large effect size). The Effort-Recovery model is also supported if the recovery is accounted for in terms of engaging in an activity conceptually different from work tasks or indeed simply allowing homeostasis to restore following the passage of time and acquisition of resources to offset future loss.

In support of our fourth hypothesis, sleep appears to be crucial to daily recovery from strain, i.e., it is significantly negatively related to fatigue scores. It was discovered that the better participants felt immediately upon arising and the more positive the ratings of the sleep episode, the less likely one is to experience fatigue at the end of the workday. Extensive research has previously confirmed the importance of sleep with regards to maintaining optimal performance (Campbell, 1992), preserving memory (Tilley & Brown, 1992), and cerebral functions (Horne, 2001; Jouvet, 1999); sleep in the present research, moreover its *quality* rather than *amount* of sleep, emerges as important to recovery. Analysis revealed that after accounting for work variables and intervening activities, sleep quality predicts recovery by reducing the experience of fatigue. It was also discovered that there were no significant differences in recovery when accounting for the duration of a sleep episode; this variable also failed to predict recovery. Thus similar to previous findings that sleep quality can predict subjective sleepiness and mood states (such as vigour) better than simple sleep quantification (e.g., Pilcher, 2000), the subjective component of sleep in the present findings emerge as more important than sleep quantity. Exactly why individuals report better sleep quality remains unclear since a physiologic examination was not possible; correlations might suggest that similar to other findings (e.g., Horne, 2001) sleep quantity plays a role in maintaining sleep quality, and therefore affecting recovery indirectly. One aspect not accounted for by the diaries was the beneficial effect of afternoon naps in maintaining alertness and reducing fatigue.

This study confirmed the importance of the traditional weekend respite since a substantial amount of recovery occurred over Saturday and Sunday: Individuals are significantly less fatigued, with parallel significant increases in sleep quality ratings and feelings upon arising. Indeed, the trend of a sharp decline in fatigue over the weekend was statistically significant. Saturday appeared to be a particularly beneficial day for recovery with regards improved sleep—it seems entirely possible that this "pinnacle day" for recovery carries over recovery effects into Sunday, explaining why fatigue levels are lowest on this day (i.e., highest levels of recovery). These beneficial effects are attributed to a period of "time off" when the pressures of work are absent, thus allowing return to prestressor levels of functioning; evidently this level of recovery is not possible during the working week. Lowest levels of recovery at the beginning of the week appear to contradict the respite effect since fatigue may be expected to be lower immediately after "time off": This can be explained in terms of "fade out". Westman and Eden (1997) found that subsequent to a vacation, burnout returned towards prevacation levels within three days; in the present case we suggest that the same mechanisms (i.e., effort-recovery) operate over the weekend, yet since this respite is only 2 days and a vacation typically much longer, this shorter duration accounts for a rapid return to highest stress (fatigue) levels. The weekend respite still operates but fades rapidly in the course of work schedules (Fritz & Sonnentag, 2005; Strauss-Blasche, Muhry, Lehofer, Moser, & Marktl, 2004). Significantly, higher fatigue scores during the weekend are related to higher fatigue on Monday; the suggestion is that if individuals are not fully recovered over the weekend, there might still be fatigue residuals on Monday. This will result in extra effort having to be exerted at the beginning of the successive week; the short-term load reactions of exerting this extra effort during Monday is evidenced by the higher fatigue scores on that evening. These results are indicative of the "vicious cycle" described by previous authors, e.g., Meijman and Mulder (1998) and Sluiter et al. (1999). Tentatively one could hypothesize that the long-term effects of insufficient recovery, such as chronic fatigue or burnout, might only manifest themselves after a long period of these cycles and poor short-term recovery; future research would seek to confirm these effects, but the trend has been elucidated.

It is interesting to note that sleep quality ratings on Monday were quite low. These ratings were obtained on Monday morning and reflect the Sunday's sleep episode. This could point in the direction of an anticipation of work demands. People start thinking of their work on Sunday evening, and start to worry, which subsequently affects their sleep quality. Indeed, our findings of anticipation of work demands and a "fade out" of respite effects is supported by recent medical research that has demonstrated a Monday morning surge in blood pressure that is associated with significant increases in deleterious cardiovascular events on Mondays, such as myocardial infarctions and strokes (Murakami et al., 2004). Thus, the recovery trends in our data are borne out by research that lends credence to the idea of a stressful change from weekend leisure activities to work activities on Monday that require mental and physical exertion. Individuals are reactivated on Mondays, both in a physiological and psychological sense.

Work variables of working time and travel time remained nonsignificant to aspects of recovery from fatigue. Although their trends are in line with the traditional working week and weekend respite, they exerted no significant effects on the outcome hypothesized variables in the study. Higher job strain was significantly negatively related to fatigue and time spent on low-effort activities: These findings seem strange in light of established links between job strain and stress reactions (e.g., Jones & Bright, 2001) and recent research demonstrating that job strain increases fatigue (Bültmann et al., 2002a). This anomaly is explicable in terms of "eustress" (Selye, 1976) and adaptive levels of "high activity" (Schabraq, Cooper, Travers, & van Maanen, 2001). Individuals may agree with statements pertaining to demands in their work (i.e., "the pace of work in my job is very intense") yet not suffer short-term reactions. One imagines healthy workers doing a "tough" day's work, with high levels of stress hormones circulating, yet during leisure time successfully return to prestressor levels. If this were the case, they wouldn't report high levels of fatigue and could conversely report increases in recovery if they feel satisfied with the day's work or experience "positive pressure". The finding that increased job strain is related to better sleep quality supports this theorizing. By enhancing self-esteem and producing satisfaction with achievement of goals (Furnham, 1997), a "hard" day at work (i.e., *active jobs*) need not result in negative reactions. Clearly, the long-term effects of job strain are unlikely to be detected by this "snapshot" into recovery processes (e.g., cardiovascular disease; Karasek & Theorell, 1990). Since respondents were not "statistically" high strain, our interpretation might be that these workers don't require low-effort recovery, thus explaining the absence of effect.

Although males and females, old and young, married and single respondents pursue different leisure patterns, these characteristics do not differentiate them in terms of recovery. Whilst it would be interesting to create recovery profiles for certain groups, analyses revealed that a demographic model was not suitable for the prediction of recovery.

Study limitations

Several methodological issues need to be accounted for when interpreting our results. The sample size is relatively small in comparison to previous diary studies and therefore cannot be regarded as truly representative of the working population in the UK.

Control over when and where respondents completed sections of the diary remains problematic. It is impossible to conclude with any certainty whether respondents completed the sleep diaries shortly after arising, or whether the CIS was completed 30 minutes before retiring. Such issues present a challenge for future research: It is now possible to equip respondents with pagers or beepers to ensure regular responses and experimental intervals, or to consider the use of electronic diaries similar to those utilized in clinical trials. This would be a move towards the experience sampling method (ESM) that would allow tighter control and a good method of studying the experience of recovery activities and the concurrent measurement of recovery variables using electronic equipment. Reactance is another problem with the validity of results since keeping a diary could alter behaviour, thoughts, and feelings (Breakwell & Wood, 2000); however, it has been suggested that leisure patterns are unlikely to be changed over such a short period (cf. Sonnentag, 2001). Nevertheless diary studies can be considered a useful method in this type of research.

Individual differences were not controlled for in this study. Dispositional factors such as Type A and B behaviour or negative affectivity are known to moderate reactions to stress (Jones & Bright, 2001) and could therefore influence fatigue scores and recovery. For example, Type A individuals who are job focused and achievement orientated could exhibit higher job strain scores. The anomaly related to job strain in the present thesis could be due to an absence of Type A individuals.

Practical implications

Several applied aspects emerge from this research. Firstly, it is suggested that individuals and organizations pay more attention to the issue of recovery outside the workplace; organizations seem reluctant to become involved in nonwork life (O'Driscoll & Cooper, 2002) but clearly nonwork time is necessary for individual recovery, without which individual and organizational "health" will suffer (Sonnentag, 2002). Occupational health should not just include work and organizational conditions, but also work – life balance and the challenges people face outside of the work domain. Interventions based on the present results will depend upon readers' personal evaluations, but several recommendations could be made. Firstly, physical activity seems to be a core aspect of recovery, particularly from the mentally demanding work faced by most individuals (Donkin, 2001). Individuals should maximize time spent on physical pursuits. Secondly, the weekend is a period that organizations should "preserve" in order to allow employees to recover; whilst this tradition is not overtly threatened, the increase in mobile technology and rapid communication devices means that individuals are more likely to engage the same psychological systems when not at work, or perhaps when "recovering" (e.g., Zijlstra et al., 1996). Direct intervention to improve sleep quality is also important—one possibility may be to ensure that work tasks or problems have received a degree of "closure" prior to leaving the work setting, thus ensuring that individuals do not "activate" themselves subsequently. Organizations might also consider paying particular attention to these issues on Monday, particularly when recovery over the medium-term, and possibly long-term, will depend upon psychological states on this day.

Implications for future research

Future research into daily recovery could make use of the present diaries, perhaps triangulating results with additional measures of recovery such as situational well-being. Longitudinal research could confirm the long-term structure of recovery activities and elucidate cumulative cycle effects. To supplement psychological variables, one could also include some physiological indices of recovery (e.g., blood pressure, heart rate, hormone secretions), mapping objective proxies of the recovery process against self-reports. A physiological examination of sleep (e.g., "activity watches" to monitor nocturnal movements) may help to elucidate aspects that enhance sleep quality. Baseline and control measures of fatigue taken shortly after returning to the home setting were not obtained due to concerns about order effects, an excess of data and the suitability of the CIS for such use. However, control scores of recovery at the end of the workday would allow more precise isolation of the effects of recovery activities when compared to scores taken before going to bed. An additional way to expand upon the present research is to use comparison groups of respondents from the same organization, with the same work roles: one group including employees with tendencies towards low-effort recovery and sedentary lifestyles, whilst the latter would include individuals who engage in physical and active leisure; rates of recovery could then be compared.

CONCLUSION

This study demonstrated that it is necessary to look at general lifestyle patterns (including leisure and sleep) if one wants to understand the effects of job stressors on peoples' health. Recovery from daily strain is determined by the work – rest cycle. What constitutes successful recovery may ultimately differ across individuals. Only through replications will psychologists arrive at a more precise understanding of what constitutes successful recovery on the fatigue continuum. Replications with a larger sample are strongly recommended, which could help elucidate cut-off points for recovery, i.e., scores that represent successful recovery. Perhaps what emerges is that stress and our adaptation to it (i.e., fatigue) is an individual process. Individuals need to discover their own thresholds and live at a pace of life suited to their needs: For Selye (1976, p. 413), "Activity and rest must be judiciously balanced, and every person has his own characteristic requirements for rest and activity." Some individuals may maintain health and avoid deleterious outcomes by taking regular short breaks or holidays (Cartwright & Cooper, 1997); others may require episodes of recovery on a daily basis involving physical activity. If individuals recognize that a bout of physical activity prepares them for rest and sleep, or conversely that they become "activated" and fatigued by completing work tasks, they should adopt strategies or reach compromises with employers to enable them to achieve a personal balance.

REFERENCES

Åkerstedt, T., Knutsson, A., Westerholm, P., Theorell, T., Alfredsson, L., & Kecklund, G. (2002). Sleep disturbances, work stress and work hours: A cross-sectional study. *Journal of Psychosomatic Research, 53,* 741 – 748.

Beurskens, A. J. H. M., Bültmann, U., Kant, I., Vercoulen, J. H. M. M., Bleijenberg, G., & Swaen, G. M. H. (2000). Fatigue among working people: Validity of a questionnaire measure. *Occupational and Environmental Medicine, 57,* 353 – 357.

Breakwell, G. M., & Wood, P. (2000). Diary techniques. In G. M. Breakwell, S. Hammond, & C. Fife-Schaw (Eds.) *Research methods in psychology* (2nd ed., pp. 294 – 302). London: Sage.

Bültmann, U. (2002). *Fatigue and psychological distress in the working population: The role of work and lifestyle.* Maastricht, The Netherlands: Universitaire Pers Maastricht.

Bültmann, U., de Vries, M., Beurskens, A. J. H. M., Bleijenberg, G., Vercoulen, J. H. M. M., & Kant, I. (2000). Measurement of prolonged fatigue in the working population: Determination of a cutoff point for the checklist individual strength. *Journal of Occupational Health Psychology, 5*(4), 411 – 416.

Bültmann, U., Kant, I., Kasl, S., Beurskens, A. J. H. M., & van den Brandt, P. A. (2002a). Fatigue and psychological distress in the working population: Psychometrics, prevalence, and correlates. *Journal of Psychosomatic Research, 52*(6), 445 – 452.

Bültmann, U., Kant, I., Kasl, S. V., Schroer, K. A. P., Swaen, G. M. H., & van den Brandt, P. A. (2002b). Lifestyle factors as risk factors for fatigue and psychological distress in the working population: Prospective results from the Maastricht Cohort Study. *Journal of Occupational and Environmental Medicine, 44,* 116–124.

Campbell, S. S. (1992). Effects of sleep and circadian rhythms of performance. In A. P. Smith & D. M. Jones (Eds.), *Handbook of human performance: Vol. 3. State and trait* (pp. 195–235). London: Academic Press.

Cartwright, S., & Cooper, C. L. (1997). *Managing workplace stress.* London: Sage.

Coakes, S. J., & Steed, L. G. (2001). *SPSS analysis without anguish.* Chichester, UK: Wiley.

Confederation of British Industry [CBI]. (2001). *Healthcare brief: Business and healthcare for the 21st century.* London: Author.

Craig, A., & Cooper, R. E. (1992). Symptoms of acute and chronic fatigue. In A. P. Smith & D. M. Jones (Eds.), *Handbook of human performance: Vol. 3. State and trait* (pp. 289–339). London: Academic Press.

Cropley, M., Steptoe, A., & Joekes, K. (1999). Job strain and psychiatric morbidity. *Psychological Medicine, 29,* 1411–1416.

Department for Work and Pensions [DWP]. (2002). *Pathways to work: helping people into employment* [Green Paper]. London: Author.

Donkin, R. (2001). *Blood, sweat and tears: The evolution of work.* New York: Texere.

Eden, D. (2001). Vacations and other respites: Studying stress on and off the job. In C. L. Cooper & I. T. Robertson (Eds.), *Well-being in organisations: A reader for students and practitioners* (pp. 121–146). Chichester, UK: Wiley.

Etzion, D., Eden, D., & Lapidot, Y. (1998). Relief from job stressors and burnout: Reserve service as a respite. *Journal of Applied Psychology, 83*(4), 577–585.

Evans, O., & Steptoe, A. (2001). Social support at work, heart rate, and cortisol: A self-monitoring study. *Journal of Occupational Health Psychology, 6*(4), 361–370.

Frankenhaeuser, M. (1989). A biopsychosocial approach to work life issues. *International Journal of Health Services, 19,* 747–758.

Frankenhaeuser, M., Lundberg, U., Fredrikson, M., Melin, B., Tuomisto, M., Myrsten, A.-L., et al. (1989). Stress on and off the job as related to sex and occupational status in white-collar workers. *Journal of Organizational Behavior, 10,* 321–346.

Fritz, C., & Sonnentag, S. (2005). Recovery, health, and job performance: Effects of weekend experiences. *Journal of Occupational Health Psychology, 10,* 187–199.

Furnham, A. (1997). *The psychology of behaviour at work: The individual in the organisation.* Hove, UK: Psychology Press.

Harris, C., Daniels, K., & Briner, R. B. (2003). A daily diary study of goals and affective well-being at work. *Journal of Occupational and Organizational Psychology, 76*(3), 401–410.

Hobfoll, S. E., & Shirom, A. (2001). Conservation of resources theory: Applications to stress and management in the workplace. In R. T. Golembiewski (Ed.), *Handbook of organizational behavior* (2nd ed., pp. 57–80). New York: Marcel Dekker.

Horne, J. A. (2001). State of the art: Sleep. *The Psychologist, 14*(6), 302–306.

Hull, B. R. (1990). Mood as a product of leisure: Causes and consequences. *Journal of Leisure Research, 22*(2), 99–111.

Iso-Ahola, S. E. (1997). A psychological analysis of leisure and health. In J. T. Haworth (Ed.), *Work, leisure and well-being* (pp. 131–144). London: Routledge.

Iwasaki, Y. (2001). Contributions of leisure to coping with daily hassles in university students' lives. *Canadian Journal of Behavioural Science, 33*(2), 128–141.

Jette, M. (1997). Stress coping through physical activity. In A. S. Sethi & R. S. Schuler (Eds.), *Handbook of organisational stress coping strategies* (pp. 84–103). Cambridge, MA: Ballinger.

Johns, M. W., & Dore, C. (1978). Sleep at home and in the sleep laboratory: Disturbance by recording procedures. *Ergonomics, 21*(5), 325–330.

Jones, F., & Bright, J. (Eds.). (2001). *Stress: Myth, theory and research.* Upper Saddle River, NJ: Prentice Hall.

Josten, E. (2002). *The effects of extended workdays* (PhD thesis, Tilburg University). Assen, The Netherlands: VanGorcum Publishers.

Jouvet, M. (1999). *The paradox of sleep: The story of dreaming.* London: MIT Press.

Karasek, R. A. (1979). Job demands, job decision latitude and mental strain: Implications for job redesign. *Administrative Science Quarterly, 24,* 285–308.

Karasek, R. T., & Theorell, T. (1990). *Healthy work, stress and productivity in working life.* New York: Basic Books.

Killen, J. D., George, J., Marchini, E., Silverman, S., & Thoresen, C. (1982). Estimating sleep parameters: A multitrait-multimethod analysis. *Journal of Consulting and Clinical Psychology, 50*(3), 345–352.

Kompier, M. A. J. (1988). *Work and health of city bus drivers.* Delft, The Netherlands: Eburon.

Landsbergis, P. A. (2003). The changing organization of work and the safety and health of working people: A commentary. *Journal of Occupational and Environmental Medicine, 45*(1), 61–72.

Meijman, T. F. (1991). *Over Vermoeidheid* [Over fatigued; Psychological studies on perception of workload effects]. Unpublished PhD thesis, Groningen University, The Netherlands.

Meijman, T. F., & Mulder, G. (1998). Psychological aspects of workload. In P. J. D. Drenth, H. Thierry, & C. J. deWolff (Eds.), *Handbook of work and organisational psychology: Vol. 2. Work psychology* (2nd ed., pp. 5–33). Hove, UK: Psychology Press.

Mikulincer, M., Babkoff, H., Caspy, T., & Sing, H. (1989). The effects of 72 hours of sleep loss on psychological variables. *British Journal of Psychology, 80,* 145–162.

Moncrieff, J., & Pomerleau, J. (2000). Trends in sickness benefits in Great Britain and the contribution of mental disorders. *Journal of Public Health Medicine, 22*(1), 59–67.

Morin, C. M. (1993). *Insomnia: Psychological assessment and management.* London: Guilford Press.

Murakami, S., Otsuka, K., Kubo, Y., Shinagawa, M., Yamanaka, T., Ohkawa, S., & Kitaura, Y. (2004). Repeated ambulatory monitoring reveals a Monday morning surge in blood pressure in a community-dwelling population. *American Journal of Hypertension, 17,* 1179–1183.

O'Driscoll, M. P., & Cooper, C. L. (2002). Job-related stress and burnout. In P. Warr (Ed.), *Psychology at work* (5th ed.). London: Penguin.

Office for National Statistics. (1998). Average hours usually worked per week by full-time employees: By gender, EU comparison, 1998, *Social Trends, 30.* Dataset: ST30418. Retrieved June 25, 2002, from http://www.statistics.gov.uk/statbase

Pawlikowska, T., Chalder, T., Hirsch, S. R., Wallace, P., Wright, D. J. M., & Wessely, S. C. (1994). Population based study of fatigue and psychological distress. *British Medical Journal, 308,* 763–766.

Pilcher, J. J. (2000). Self-report sleep habits as predictors of subjective sleepiness. *Behavioural Medicine,* Winter. Retrieved 6 December 2001, from http://www.findarticles.com

Ray, C., Weir, W. R. C., Cullen, S., & Phillips, S. (1992). Illness perception and symptom components in chronic fatigue syndrome. *Journal of Psychosomatic Research, 36*(3), 243–256.

Roe, R. A., van den Berg, P. T., Zijlstra, F. R. H., Schalk, M. J. D., Taillieu, T. C. B., & van der Wielen, J. M. M. (1994). New concepts for a new age: Information service organizations and mental information work. *The European Work and Organizational Psychologist, 3*(2), 177–192.

Rystedt, L. W., Johansson, G., & Evans, G. W. (1998). A longitudinal study of workload, health and well-being among male and female urban bus drivers. *Journal of Occupational and Organisational Psychology, 71,* 35–45.

Schabracq, M., Cooper, C., Travers, C., & van Maanen, D. (2001). *Occupational health psychology: The challenge of workplace stress.* Leicester, UK: BPS Books.

Selye, H. (1976). *The stress of life.* New York: McGraw-Hill.

Sluiter, J. K. (1999). *How about work demands, recovery and health? A neuro-endocrine field study during and after work* (PhD thesis). Amsterdam, The Netherlands: Studie Centrum Arbeid en Gezondheid, Academisch Medisch Centrum.

Sluiter, J. K., Frings-Dresen, M. H. W., van der Beek, A. J., & Meijman, T. F. (2001). The relation between work-induced neuroendocrine reactivity and recovery, subjective need for recovery, and health status. *Journal of Psychosomatic Research, 50,* 29–37.

Sluiter, J. K., van der Beek, A. J., & Frings-Dresen, M. H. W. (1999). The influence of workload on the need for recovery and experienced health: A study on coach drivers. *Ergonomics, 42*(4), 573–583.

Sonnentag, S. (2000). *Assessing daily recovery activities: First experiences with a diary method* (Tech. Rep.). Konstanz, Germany: University of Konstanz.

Sonnentag, S. (2001). Work, recovery activities, and individual well-being: A diary study. *Journal of Occupational Health Psychology, 6*(3), 196–210.

Sonnentag, S. (2003). Recovery, work engagement and proactive behaviour: A new look at the interface between nonwork and work. *Journal of Applied Psychology, 88*(3), 518–528.

Spurgeon, A., & Cooper, C. L. (2000). Working time, mental health and performance. In C. L. Cooper & I. T. Robertson (Eds.), *International review of industrial and organisational psychology* (Vol. 15). Chichester, UK: Wiley.

Steinberg, H., Nicholls, B. R., Sykes, E. A., LeBoutillier, N., Ramlakhan, N., Moss, T. P., & Dewey, A. (1998). Weekly exercise consistently reinstates positive mood. *The European Psychologist, 3*(4), 271–280.

Strauss-Blasche, G., Muhry, F., Lehofer, M., Moser, M., & Marktl, W. (2004). Time course of well-being after a three-week resort-based respite from occupational and domestic demands: Carry-over, contrast and situation effects. *Journal of Leisure Research, 36*(3), 293–309.

Tabachnick, B. G., & Fidell, L. S. (2001). *Using multivariate statistics* (4th ed.). Needham Heights, AL: Allyn & Bacon.

Tilley, A. J., & Brown, S. (1992). Sleep deprivation. In A. P. Smith & D. M. Jones (Eds.), *Handbook of human performance: Vol. 3. State and trait* (pp. 237–288). London: Academic Press.

Vercoulen, J. H. M. M., Swanink, C. M. A., Fennis, J. F. M., Galma, J. M. D., van der Meer, J. W. M., & Bleijenberg, G. (1994). Dimensional assessment of chronic fatigue syndrome. *Journal of Psychosomatic Research, 38*(5), 383–392.

Westman, M., & Eden, D. (1997). Effects of a respite from work on burnout: Vacation relief and fade-out. *Journal of Applied Psychology, 82*(4), 516–527.

Westman, M., & Etzion, D. (2001). The impact of vacation and job stress on burnout and absenteeism. *Psychology and Health, 16,* 595–606.

Zijlstra, F. R. H. (1993). *Efficiency in work behaviour: A design approach for modern tools* (PhD thesis, Delft University of Technology). Delft, The Netherlands: Delft University Press.

Zijlstra, F. R. H., & de Vries, J. (2000). Burnout en de bijdrage van socio-demografische en werkgebonden variabelen [Burnout and the contribution of socio-demographic and work-related variables]. In I. L. D. Houtman, W. B. Schaufeli, & T. Taris (Eds.), *Psychische Vermoeidheid en Werk: Cijfers, trends en analyses* (pp. 83–95). Alphen a/d. Rijn, \the Netherlands: Samsom.

Zijlstra, F. R. H., Schalk, M. J. D., & Roe, R. A. (1996). Veranderingen in de Arbeid. Consequenties voor Werkenden [Changes in work: Consequences for working people]. *Tijdschrift voor Arbeidsvraagstukken, 12*(3), 251–263.